Carefully cut out the clock and hands. Put them together. Write your name on the back.

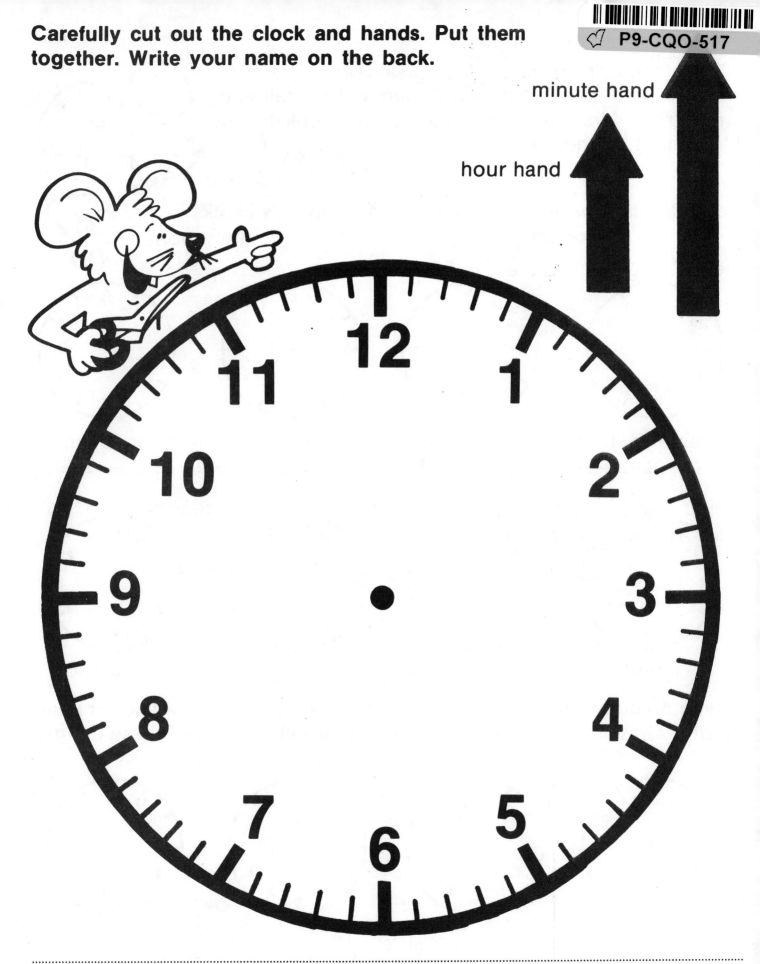

minute hand

hour hand

Teacher: Use with pages 5, 6, 9, 15, 16, 17, 18, 19. See page 105 for further instructions on how to use this page.

© Frank Schaffer Publications, Inc.   1   FS-32021 Math Activities

"Here's your new puppy, Andy," said Mrs. Nelson. "I hope you will take good care of him. Let me tell you what to do." Mrs. Nelson wrote a list. Andy took it home. He hung it on the wall.

Read the time words. Draw the hands on Andy's clocks.

Morning

seven

breakfast

nine

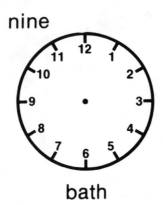

bath

Afternoon

ten

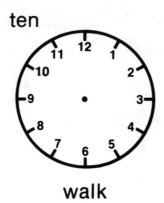

walk

four

brush fur

══ Evening ══

six

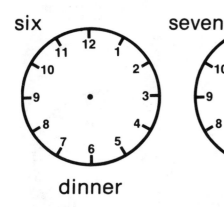

dinner

seven

walk

nine

read a story

eleven

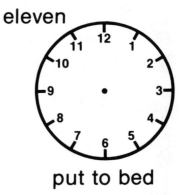

put to bed

Pretend you have a pet gorilla. Write four things you would do for your gorilla. Draw the hands to show when you will do each of these things.

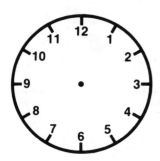

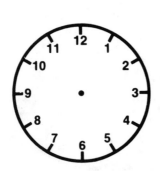

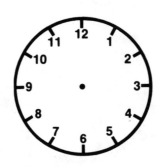

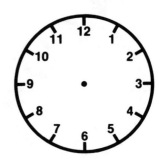

2 FS-32021 Math Activities

Hour hand

one hour

Minute hand

one minute

There are 60 minutes in one hour.

The hour is three o'clock or 3:00.

Fill in the missing hands.

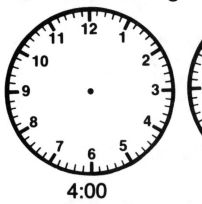

4:00

11:00

7:00

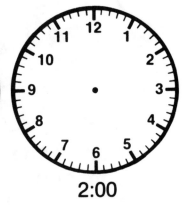

2:00

Read the time under each clock. Draw the hands correctly. Write the new time on the line.

 _____

two hours after 10

 _____

five hours after 6

one hour after 9

three hours after 2

 _____

one hour before 11

 _____

four hours before 4

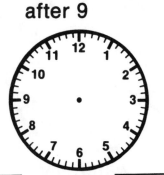 _____

six hours before 10

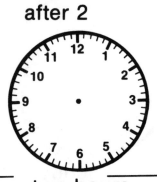 _____

two hours before 2

3

Name _____

"The show starts at nine o'clock," Ann told her mother. "Is that nine in the morning?"

"Yes, it is," answered Mother. "Do you know how to tell? Look at the letters after nine. It says a.m. That means 'in the morning'. There are twelve morning hours—midnight to twelve noon.

"Another show starts at eight p.m. P.M. means 'in the afternoon or evening'. There are twelve p.m. hours—twelve noon to midnight. Each day has 24 hours."

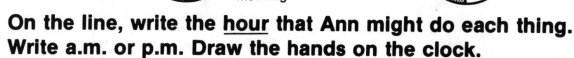

Morning   Early Morning   Evening   Afternoon

On the line, write the _hour_ that Ann might do each thing.
Write a.m. or p.m. Draw the hands on the clock.

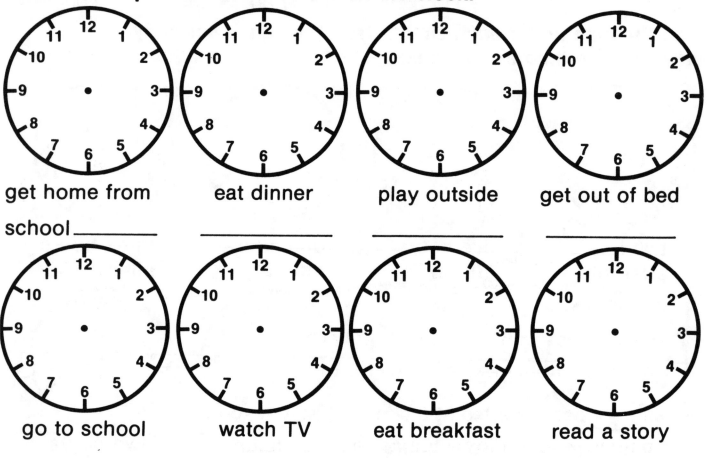

get home from school _____

eat dinner _____

play outside _____

get out of bed _____

go to school _____

watch TV _____

eat breakfast _____

read a story _____

FS-32021 Math Activities

Name _____

Get your clock. Read the sentences and write your answers.
The time is on the hour. You only need to move the small hand.

1. Sue gets up at 7 a.m. (set your clock). In one hour, she will eat breakfast. The time will be _____ .

2. Mr. Loof is coming at 2 p.m. (set). It will take him three hours to fix the TV. He will finish at _____ .

3. Dad got on the plane at 12 p.m. (set). The plane took off at 2 p.m. How many hours did Dad have to wait? _____ .

4. We are driving to Magic Land. We'll leave at 9 a.m. (set). It takes four hours to get there. What time in the afternoon will we arrive? _____

5. The sun rose at 6 a.m. (set). It set at 5 p.m. How many hours had passed? _____

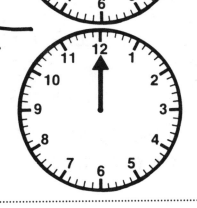

6. Jimmy's game started at 6 p.m. (set). It ended at 9 p.m. How long did the game last? _____

Name _____

Half hour = 30 minutes

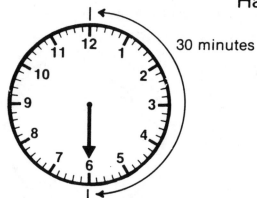

30 minutes

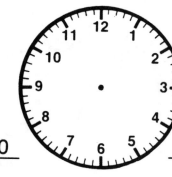

The time is 30 minutes past . . . the hour of 3 o'clock.

The time is 3:30 **or** half past 3.

Draw the hands to show the time.

7:30 _____

11:30 _____

1:30 _____

Write the correct time.

_____   _____   _____   _____

Get your clock. Answer the questions.

1. Jan ate lunch at 12 p.m. (set your clock). Half an hour later she went out to play. What time is it? _____

2. "Huckle Harry" ends at 9 p.m. (set). John goes to bed 30 minutes later. What time will it be? _____

3. Mom leaves for work at 6 a.m. (set). She gets to work half an hour later. What time is it? _____

....
Teacher: Use with the clock on page 1.

6

FS-32021 Math Activities

Name _____

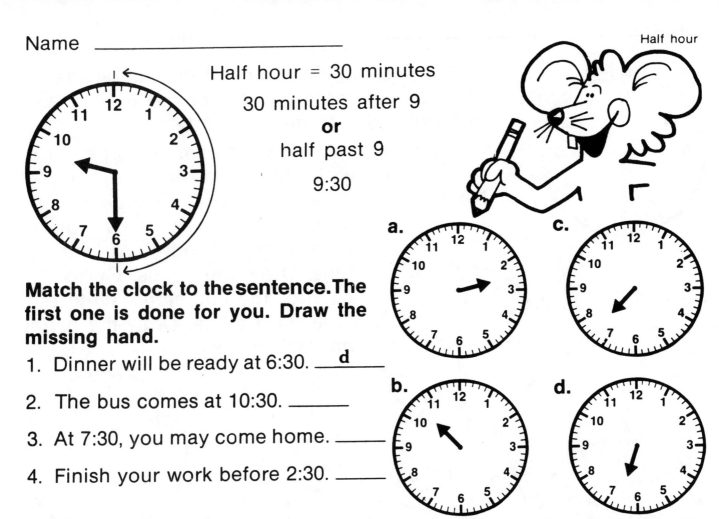

Half hour = 30 minutes

30 minutes after 9

or

half past 9

9:30

a.

c.

Match the clock to the sentence. The first one is done for you. Draw the missing hand.

1. Dinner will be ready at 6:30. ____**d**____

2. The bus comes at 10:30. _____

3. At 7:30, you may come home. _____

4. Finish your work before 2:30. _____

b.

d.

Read the sentences. Draw the hands to show the time. Later means: move the small hand ahead. Early means: move the small hand back.

5. School started at 9 a.m. John came home 30 minutes later. _____

6. The park opens at 3:00. The children arrive half an hour early. _____

7. A movie starts at 5:30. It ends 30 minutes later. _____

8. Palmer's store closes at 8 p.m. Jed's store closes half an

   hour later. _____

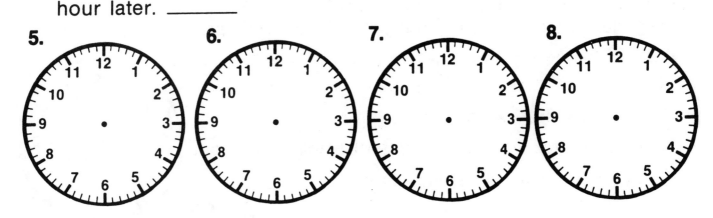

5.   **6.**   **7.**   **8.**

     FS-32021 Math Activities

Name _____

George is going to spend the day at the zoo. He will catch the "M" bus at 8 a.m. The bus will arrive at the zoo at 12 p.m.

Go to stop #1. What time will George get on the bus? Draw the hands to the right time. Next, trace the line to stop #2. It took 30 minutes for the bus to get there. What time is it now? Write the time. Draw the hands. Go to each of the bus stops. Write the time on the line. Draw the hands on each clock.

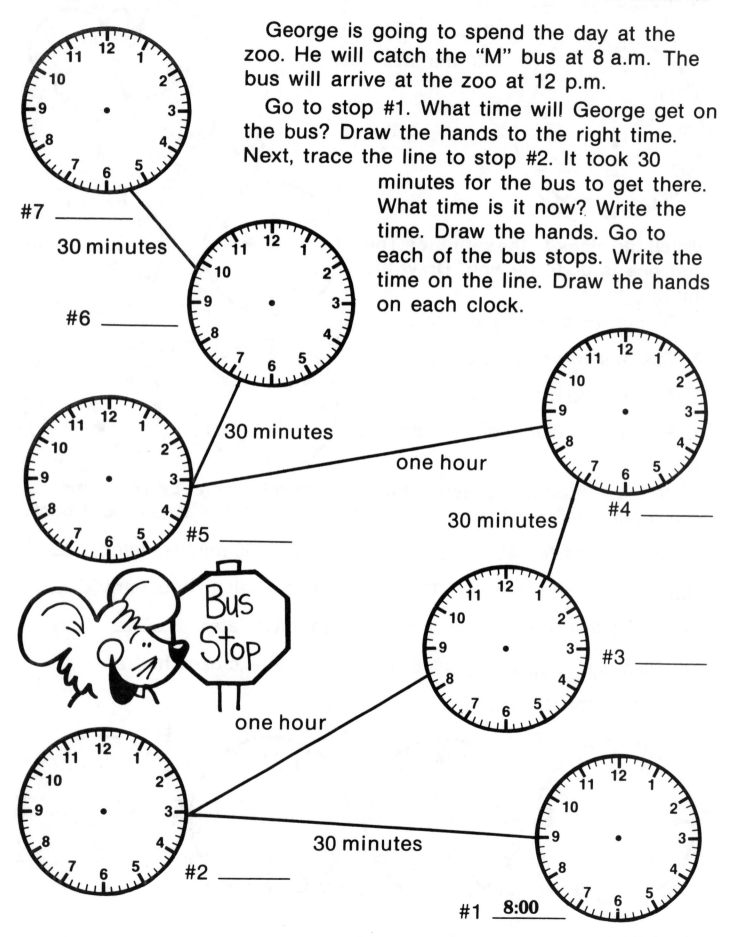

#7 _____

30 minutes

#6 _____

30 minutes

one hour

#4 _____

30 minutes

#5 _____

#3 _____

one hour

#2 _____

30 minutes

#1 __**8:00**__

Name _____

1.

2.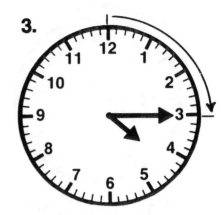

3.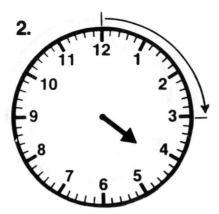

The time is
fifteen **minutes** past . . . the **hour** of four.

The time is 4:15 **OR**
quarter past four

Draw the hands to the correct time, then write the time as in clock number 3.

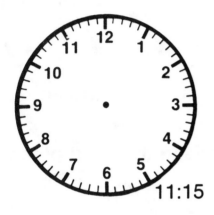
11:15

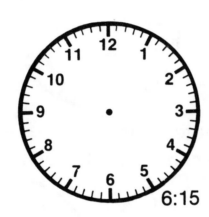
6:15

5:15

_____ _____ _____

Answer the questions using your clock.

1. Jane ate lunch at noon (set your clocks). Fifteen minutes later she took a nap. The time is _____.

2. The play started at 5:30 (set). Everyone came fifteen minutes early. What time is it? _____

3. I'm taking the bus to the dentist. It leaves at 9:15 (set). I'll arrive two hours later. The time will be: _____.

4. Mike got to the game at 6:00 (set). The game started fifteen minutes later. What time did the game start? _____

Milk

Name _____

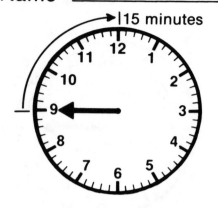

The time is fifteen
minutes **before** . . . the hour of seven   **OR** quarter to seven

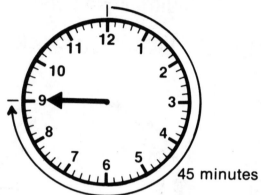

The time is 45 minutes **after** . . . the hour of six **OR** 6:45

Look at the time under each clock. Draw the hands in the right place.

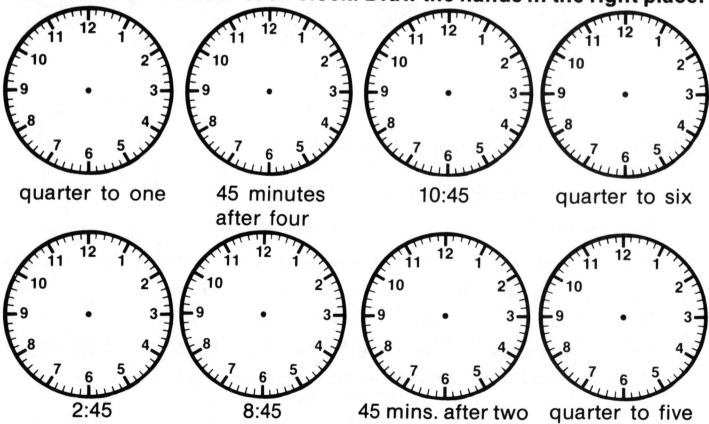

quarter to one   45 minutes   10:45   quarter to six
                      after four

2:45   8:45   45 mins. after two   quarter to five

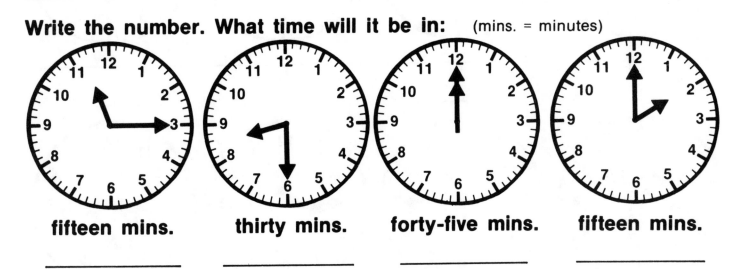

15 miniutes   30 minutes   45 minutes

4:15
quarter past 4

4:30
half past 4

4:45
quarter to 5

Write the number. What time will it be in: (mins. = minutes)

fifteen mins.   thirty mins.   forty-five mins.   fifteen mins.

_____   _____   _____   _____

Read the sentence. Find the answer in the word box below.

1. Ann ate lunch at noon. She finished in fifteen minutes: _____

2. The moon rises at 8 p.m. Steve goes to bed forty-five minutes later:

_____

3. Linda is a fast runner. She left her house at 9:00. She got to my house

thirty minutes later: _____

4. The movie starts at 11:00. It ends forty-five minutes later: _____

half past 9 • quarter to 12 • quarter past 12 • quarter to 9

Name _____

**Write the time shown on the clock: (1) quarter to; quarter past; half past.
(2) Write the time using numbers. For example:** quarter to ten - 9:45

Name _____

Write the time in numerals.

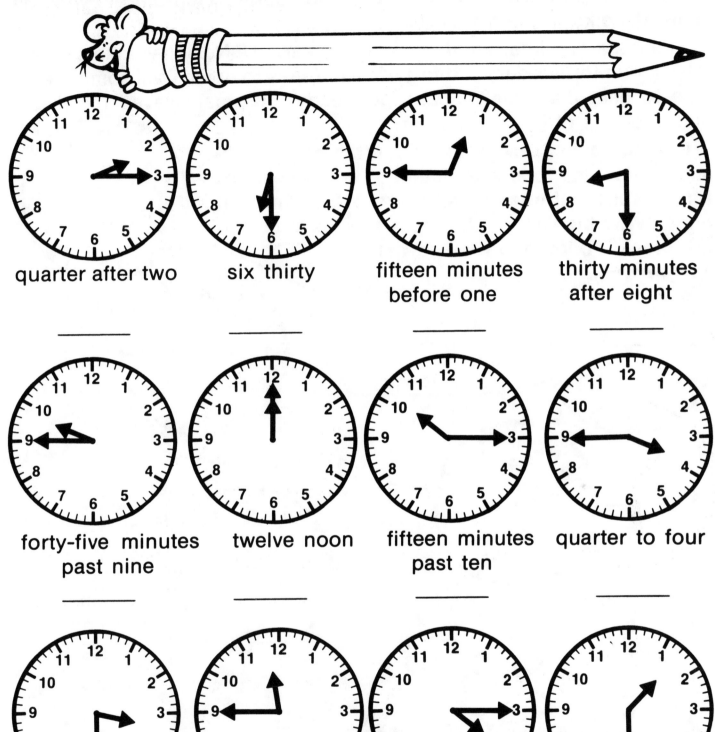

quarter after two   six thirty   fifteen minutes
before one

thirty minutes
after eight

_____   _____   _____   _____

forty-five minutes
past nine

twelve noon

fifteen minutes
past ten

quarter to four

_____   _____   _____   _____

half past three

forty-five mins.
after eleven

quarter
after four

thirty minutes
after one

_____   _____   _____   _____

13   FS-32021 Math Activities

Name _____

"The big race is tomorrow!" exclaimed Joann. "I'm going to win this year. My bike is the fastest!"

At the starting line, a man said: "Last year, Jeff Nelsen won this race. It took him three hours and forty-five minutes to finish. Will someone be able to beat that time?" Joann got ready. The man waved the flag and she was off!

Put your pencil on clock #1. Draw the hands to 10 a.m. Follow the road with Joann to the next clock. It took thirty minutes to get there. What time is it now? Write the time on the line. Draw the hands on the clock. Follow the road to the end.

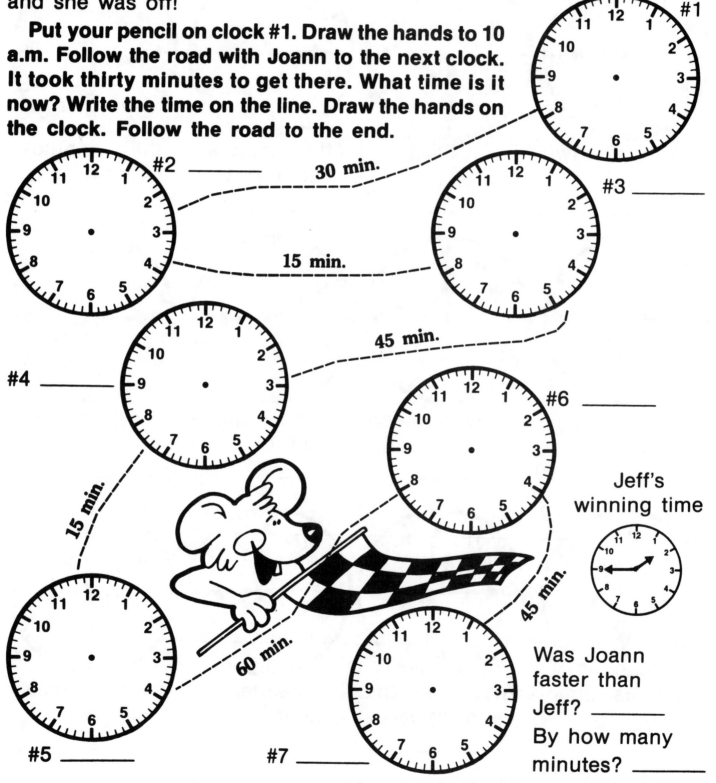

#1

#2 _____   30 min.   #3 _____

15 min.

45 min.

#4 _____

#6 _____

15 min.

Jeff's winning time

60 min.

45 min.

Was Joann faster than Jeff? _____

By how many minutes? _____

#5 _____   #7 _____

14   FS-32021 Math Activities

9:05

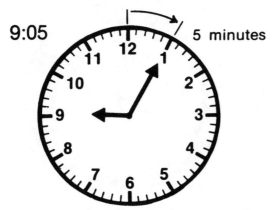

5 minutes

3:50

Count by 5's

The time is five minutes past the hour of 9.

The time is fifty minutes past the hour of 3.

Draw the missing minute hand.

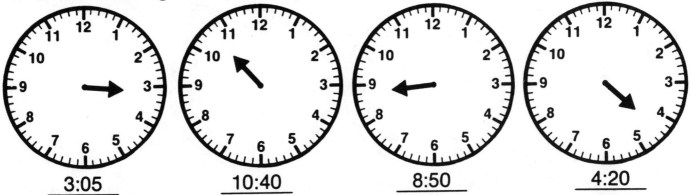

3:05　　　10:40　　　8:50　　　4:20

Set your clock hands to the time that is ★. Read the time. Move the minute hand to the new time. Fill in the clock.

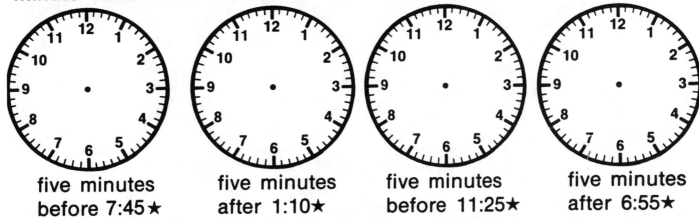

five minutes before 7:45★

five minutes after 1:10★

five minutes before 11:25★

five minutes after 6:55★

Get your clocks. Write how many minutes are there:

1. from 9:30 (set your clock) to 9:50? Count by five. _____

2. from 12:15 (set) to 12:45: Count by five. _____

3. from 2:35 (set) to 3:00? Count by five. _____

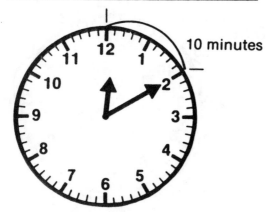

10 minutes

The time is ten minutes
past the hour of 12.

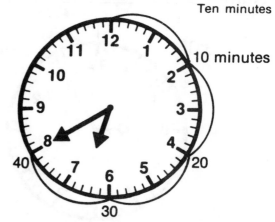

Ten minutes

10 minutes

The time is forty minutes
past the hour of 6.

Look at the time under each clock. Draw the hands in the right place.

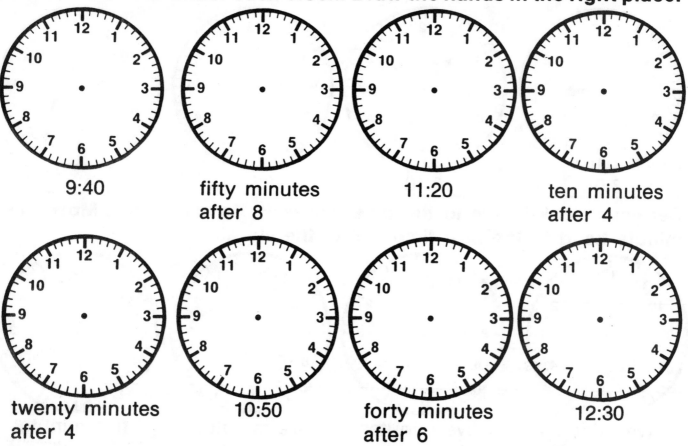

9:40

fifty minutes
after 8

11:20

ten minutes
after 4

twenty minutes
after 4

10:50

forty minutes
after 6

12:30

Get your clocks. Count by ten. Write how many minutes are there:

1. from 4:20 (set your clocks) to 4:50? _____

2. from 11:40 (set) to 12:20? _____

3. from 7:50 to (set) 8:10? _____

Teacher: Use with the clock on page 1.

FS-32021 Math Activities

Name _____

What is your school day like? Write these activities in the box in the correct order. Fill in the time you do each activity.

roll call   spelling   recess

lunch   math   science   art

p.e.   music   reading

	Activity	Starts	Ends
1.	roll call	9:00	9:15
2.			
3.			
4.			
5.			
6.			
7.			
8.			
9.			
10.			

Use your clocks. Find out how long each activity lasts. Write your answer below.

1. _____

2. _____

3. _____

4. _____

5. _____

6. _____

7. _____

8. _____

9. _____

10. _____

Teacher: Use with the clock on page 1.

17

    FS-32021 Math Activities

Name _____

**Do these clocks tell the right time? If the answer is 'yes',
write Y. If not, write the correct time on the line.**

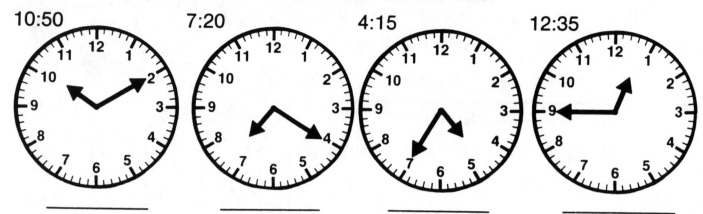

10:50   7:20   4:15   12:35

_____   _____   _____   _____

Use your clock. How many minutes is it past the hour?

_____   _____   _____   _____

Use your clock. Count by five. What time will it be in:

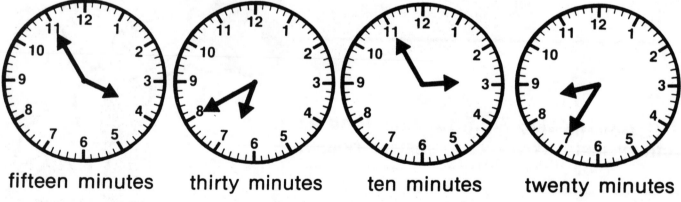

fifteen minutes   thirty minutes   ten minutes   twenty minutes

_____   _____   _____   _____

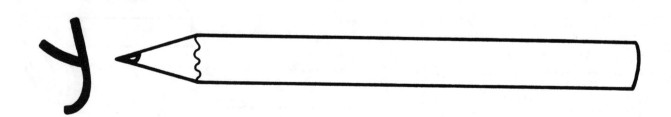

Teacher: Use with the clock on page 1.

18   FS-32021 Math Activities

Name _____

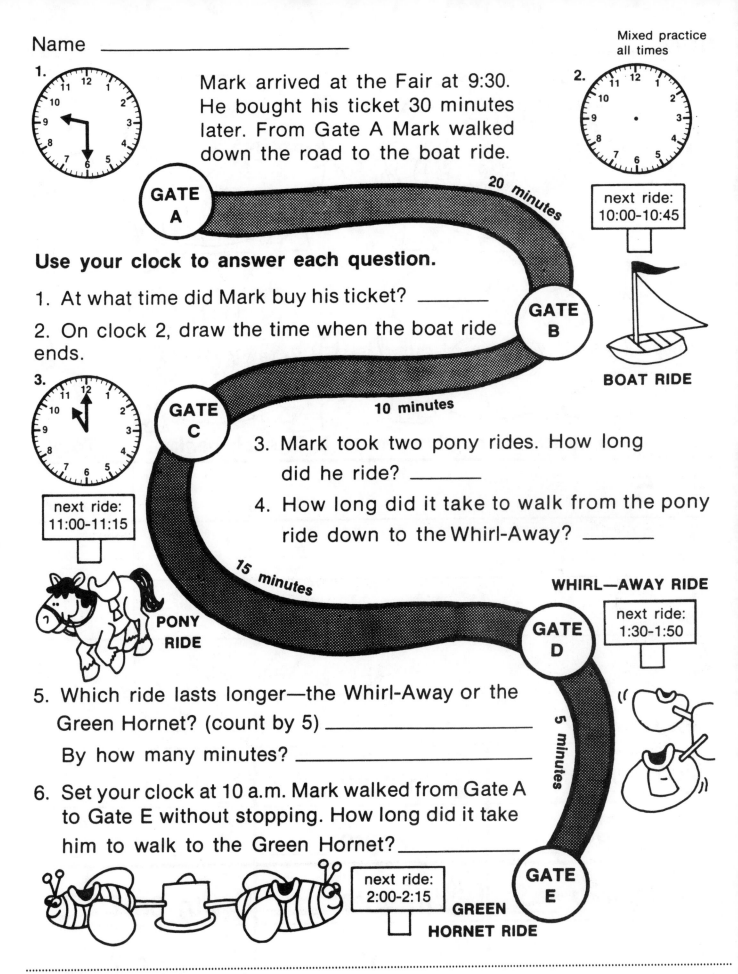

1.

Mark arrived at the Fair at 9:30. He bought his ticket 30 minutes later. From Gate A Mark walked down the road to the boat ride.

GATE A

2.

20 minutes

next ride:
10:00–10:45

BOAT RIDE

GATE B

Use your clock to answer each question.

1. At what time did Mark buy his ticket? _____

2. On clock 2, draw the time when the boat ride ends.

3.

GATE C

10 minutes

next ride:
11:00–11:15

3. Mark took two pony rides. How long did he ride? _____

4. How long did it take to walk from the pony ride down to the Whirl-Away? _____

15 minutes

PONY RIDE

WHIRL—AWAY RIDE

next ride:
1:30–1:50

GATE D

5. Which ride lasts longer—the Whirl-Away or the Green Hornet? (count by 5) _____

By how many minutes? _____

5 minutes

6. Set your clock at 10 a.m. Mark walked from Gate A to Gate E without stopping. How long did it take him to walk to the Green Hornet?_____

next ride:
2:00–2:15

GATE E

GREEN HORNET RIDE

Teacher: Use with the clock on page 1.

FS-32021 Math Activities

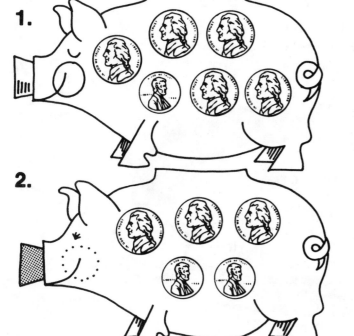

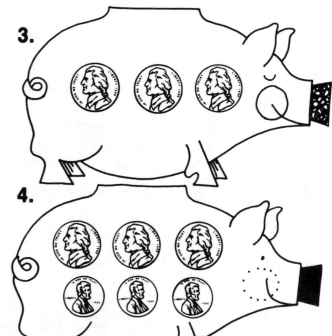

Add the coins to find out how much is in each bank.

		Total
1. 5 +	=	¢
2.	=	¢
3.	=	¢
4.	=	¢

How many:

in 25¢? ____	in 10¢? ____	in 50¢? ____
in 3¢? ____	in 8¢? ____	in 6¢? ____
in 30¢? ____	in 40¢? ____	in 35¢? ____
in 9¢? ____	in 1¢? ____	in 4¢? ____

FS-32021 Math Activities

Lisa   **Terry**

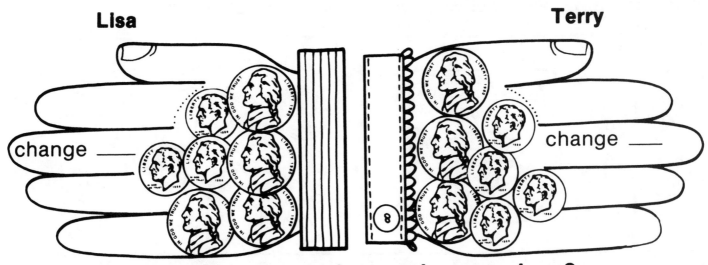

change _____   change _____

How much money does each person have?

| _____ dimes = _____¢ | **Total** |
| _____ nickels = _____¢ | _____¢ |

| _____ dimes = _____¢ | **Total** |
| _____ nickels = _____¢ | _____¢ |

Lisa and Terry are going shopping for a birthday party. When one of them buys something, put an X on the coins used.

1. Lisa bought a game.
2. Terry bought candy and a balloon.
3. Terry bought one cupcake.
4. Lisa bought one hat.

On the hands above write the change each girl has left.

5. Terry wants to buy a candle. How much more money does she

   need? _____¢

6. How much money do Lisa and Terry now have together? _____¢

7. The girls want to buy ice cream. It costs 25¢. How much more money

   will they need to buy it? _____¢

GAME 30¢   20¢   25¢   10¢   15¢   5¢

Add the coins. Find out how much each item costs.

Find the number of dimes and nickels there are in the starred (*) numbers. Add the cost. Write the price on the tag.

Dimes	Nickels
9	1

Price

* 90¢ +*5¢ = **95** ¢

Dimes	Nickels

Price

* 70¢ +*20¢ =   ¢

Dimes	Nickels

Price

* 60¢ +*10¢ =   ¢

Dimes	Nickels

Price

* 50¢ +*15¢ =   ¢

Dimes	Nickels

Price

* 30¢ +*30¢ =   ¢

FS-32021 Math Activities

 = 25¢    = 25¢   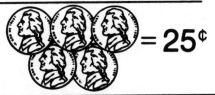 = 25¢

Tony has:

  = _____ ¢

Which coin will make 25¢?

Monica has:

 = _____ ¢

Which coin will make 25¢?

Paul has:

 = _____ ¢

Which 2 coins will make 25¢?

Kim has:

Which 3 coins will make 25¢?

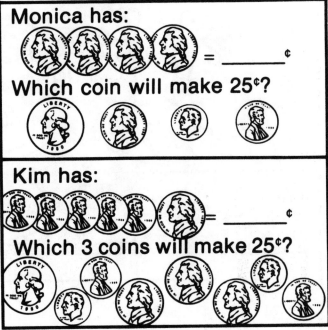

1. Monica has . She bought a . How much does she have left? _____¢

2. Paul has . He gave Kim 15¢. How much money does Paul have now? _____¢

3. Tony has . He put 25¢ in the bank. How much is left? _____¢

4. Kim wants . She has . How much more money does she need?

_____¢

5. Paul has . He wants and a . Can he buy both? _____ How much change will he have? _____¢

FS-32021 Math Activities

Can you buy:

	yes/no	more/less

1. A with a ? __no__   It costs __more__ than a .

2. A with a ? _____   It costs _____ than a .

3. A with a ? _____   It costs _____ than a .

4. A with a ? _____   It costs _____ than a .

Do you need <u>more</u> or <u>less</u> money?

5. You have  to buy a . _____

6. You have 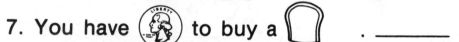 to buy a . _____

7. You have to buy a . _____

8. You have 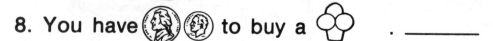 to buy a . _____

9. You have to buy a . _____

10. You have  to buy a . _____

24   FS-32021 Math Activities

Name _____

For each list, write how much is spent and how much change is left.

10¢ Buy 5.

PEAS

Cost: _____ ¢ Change: _____ ¢

25¢ Buy 2.

MILK

Cost: _____ ¢ Change: _____ ¢

5¢ Buy 5.

GUM

Cost: _____ ¢ Change: _____ ¢

25¢ Buy 3.

Cost: _____ ¢ Change: _____ ¢

5¢ Buy 8.

Cost: _____ ¢ Change: _____ ¢

10¢ Buy 9.

Cookies

Cost: _____ ¢ Change: _____ ¢

25¢ Buy 2.

Cost: _____ ¢ Change: _____ ¢

10¢ Buy 4.

Cost: _____ ¢ Change: _____ ¢

20¢ Buy 3.

Cost: _____ ¢ Change: _____ ¢

FS-32021 Math Activities

Name _____

The Bailey family went out to dinner at Don's Deli. They all chose what they wanted in their sandwiches. Add the cost of each sandwich. Follow the example.

Deli Case

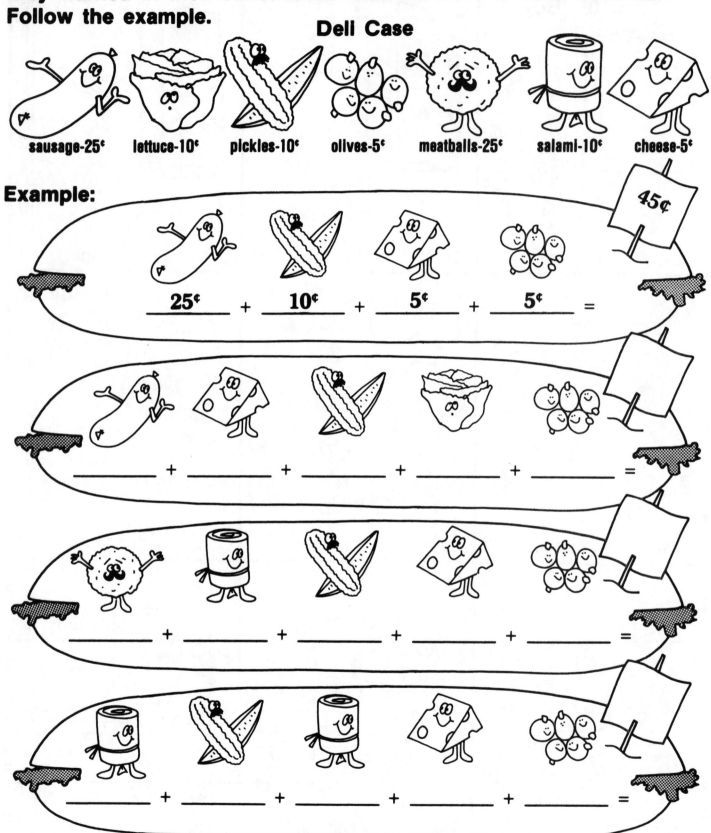

sausage-25¢   lettuce-10¢   pickles-10¢   olives-5¢   meatballs-25¢   salami-10¢   cheese-5¢

Example:

45¢

_____25¢_____ + _____10¢_____ + _____5¢_____ + _____5¢_____ =

_____ + _____ + _____ + _____ =

_____ + _____ + _____ + _____ =

_____ + _____ + _____ + _____ =

Count by 5's

= _____ ¢

Count by 10's

= _____ ¢

 = _____ ¢

Count by 25's

= _____ ¢

| | 25¢ | 45¢ | 40¢ | 50¢ | 55¢ |

| Bean Bag Toss 60¢ | | | 30¢ | 20¢ | |

Sunday at the Town Fair

(1) Put an X on the coins you will need to play each game.
(2) How much change is left?
(3) Name a food you can buy with your change.
(The box at the top will help you count.)

	1.		2.	3.
55¢				
50¢				
40¢				
Bean Bag Toss 60¢				

=50¢   =50¢   =25¢   =10¢   =5¢   =1¢

Put X's on the coins that show how much each toy costs.

Change

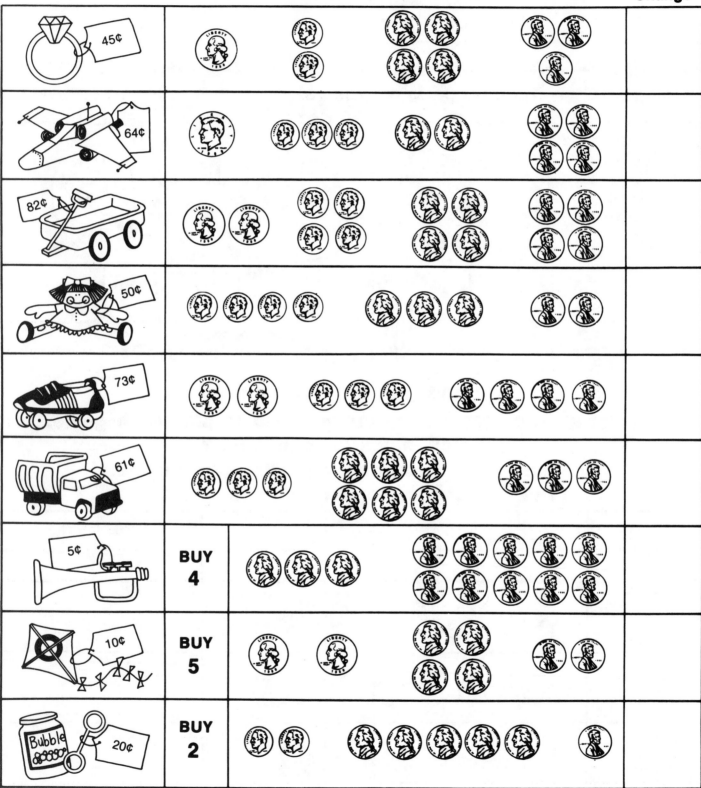

Count by 10	Count by 25	Count by 50	

____ dimes = $1.00	____ quarters = $1.00	____ half dollars = $1.00	$1.00

Each grocery order must total $1.00. (1) What coins will you need? Write Q, D, or HD on the line. (2) Write the value of each coin in the box.

Q

$\boxed{75¢}$ + $\boxed{25¢}$ = $1.00

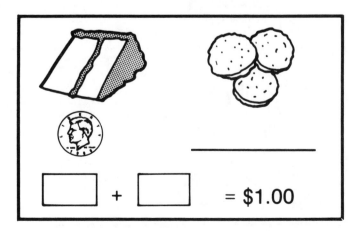

☐ + ☐ = $1.00

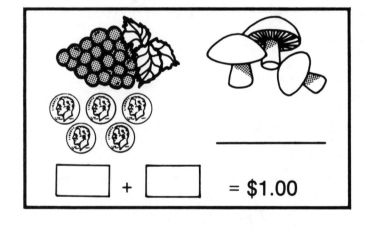

☐ + ☐ = $1.00

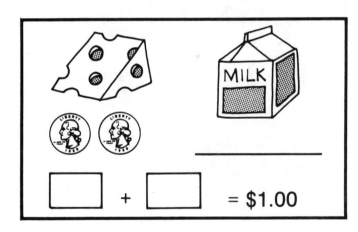

☐ + ☐ = $1.00

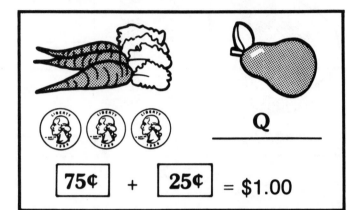

☐ + ☐ = $1.00

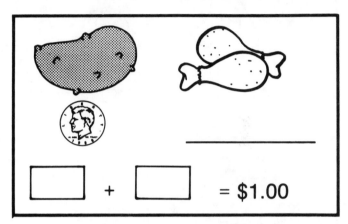

☐ + ☐ = $1.00

20 = $1.00   10  = $1.00   4 = $1.00   2  = $1.00

Write the cost of each toy. Color the toys that cost exactly $1.00.

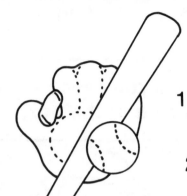

1 = _____

2 = _____

Total: _____

2 = _____

4 = _____

Total: _____

10 = _____

5 = _____

Total: _____

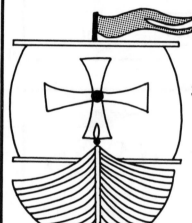

3 = _____

1 = _____

Total: _____

2 = _____

5 = _____

Total: _____

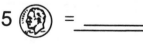

1 = _____

5 = _____

Total: _____

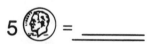

The Wacky Toy Store

25¢	5¢	5¢	10¢	25¢	5¢	5¢	10¢	25¢	1¢	1¢	10¢	10¢
a	b	c	d	e	f	g	h	i	j	k	l	m
10¢	25¢	5¢	1¢	10¢	10¢	10¢	25¢	5¢	5¢	1¢	5¢	1¢
n	o	p	q	r	s	t	u	v	w	x	y	z

The price of toys at the Wacky Toy Store depends on the letters in their names. The chart above shows what each letter is worth. Add the value of each letter to find the prices of these toys.

1. j u m p r o p e

____ ____ ____ ____ ____ ____ ____ ____

Price _____

2. y o - y o

____ ____   ____ ____

Price _____

3. f r i s b e e

____ ____ ____ ____ ____ ____ ____

Price _____

4. j a c k s

____ ____ ____ ____ ____

Price _____

5. c r a y o n s

____ ____ ____ ____ ____ ____ ____

Price _____

Brainwork! Name three toys you would like to buy. Then figure out how much they would cost at the Wacky Toy Store.

Name _____

You have	Buy	Cost	How much change do you have left?

  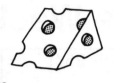

You have		**Buy**	**Cost**	**How much change do you have left?**

  $1.55   2    = $.40

MILK $ .20

  6 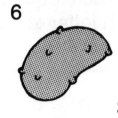 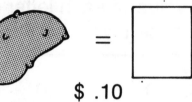 =

$ .10

  3   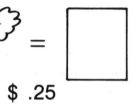 =

$ .25

 2   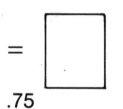 =

$ .75

  4  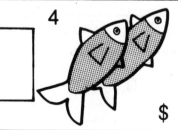 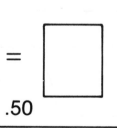 =

$ .50

  10 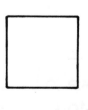 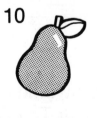 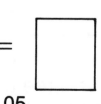 =

$ .05

FS-32021 Math Activities

Find the Numbers

Ten number words are hidden in this puzzle. The words are written across and down. Read each number below. Then find and circle its matching word or words. Write them on the blank beside the number.

A. 73 _seventy-three_   F. 12 _____

B. 91 _____   G. 18 _____

C. 60 _____   H. 39 _____

D. 56 _____   I. 20 _____

E. 80 _____   J. 44 _____

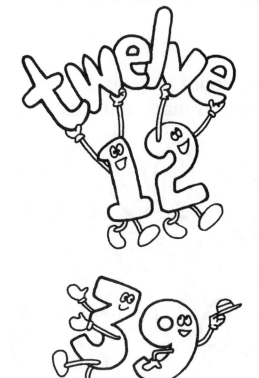

s	e	v	e	n	t	y	-	t	h	r	e	e	f
m	i	n	u	s	w	a	l	p	-	o	e	f	o
e	i	x	h	u	e	q	u	a	l	s	i	x	r
i	s	-	u	q	n	d	i	l	e	i	g	h	t
g	n	i	n	e	t	y	-	o	n	e	h	i	y
h	u	z	d	e	y	u	a	s	s	b	t	p	-
t	h	i	r	t	y	-	n	i	n	e	e	p	f
y	t	w	e	l	v	e	z	x	-	k	e	o	o
o	f	r	d	-	t	h	r	t	e	o	n	e	u
p	l	u	s	f	i	f	t	y	-	s	i	x	r

Brainwork! Find three other math words that are hidden in the puzzle. The math words match these signs: +, −, and =.

Math Maze

Count by twos to make your way through this maze to the circled number. You can move up, down, across, or diagonally one box at a time. Draw a line that shows your path.

2	4	5	24	27	30
3	6	22	23	26	29
8	9	20	28	30	32
12	10	18	31	34	33
14	16	11	36	42	45
40	39	38	40	41	(44)

5	20	26	40	31	(90)
10	35	25	30	100	85
25	15	20	35	80	81
40	45	40	76	75	95
35	46	50	61	66	70
50	61	55	60	65	76

This time count by fives. Remember to mark your path!

Brainwork! Count backwards by fives from 100 to 5. Write the numbers as you count.

FS-32021 Math Activities

Mouse Mazes

Help the mice travel through the mazes. They can move up, down, across, or diagonally one box at a time. Draw a line that shows their path.

This little mouse
   Counts by threes,
Through the maze,
   To the cheese.

	3	6	15	18	21
35	5	9	12	24	22
34	33	30	27	14	55
36	35	50	51	54	57
39	40	48	49	60	61
44	42	45	50	55	🧀

50	41	42	6	4	
47	40	14	12	8	4
45	44	36	16	20	24
61	58	48	32	28	25
66	64	50	52	53	30
🚪	61	60	56	50	35

This little mouse
   Counts by fours,
Searching for
   the double doors.

4, 8, 12...

Brainwork! Shade in the five numbers that are on both paths.

On Target

Be on target with your addition facts. In each box write the missing sum.

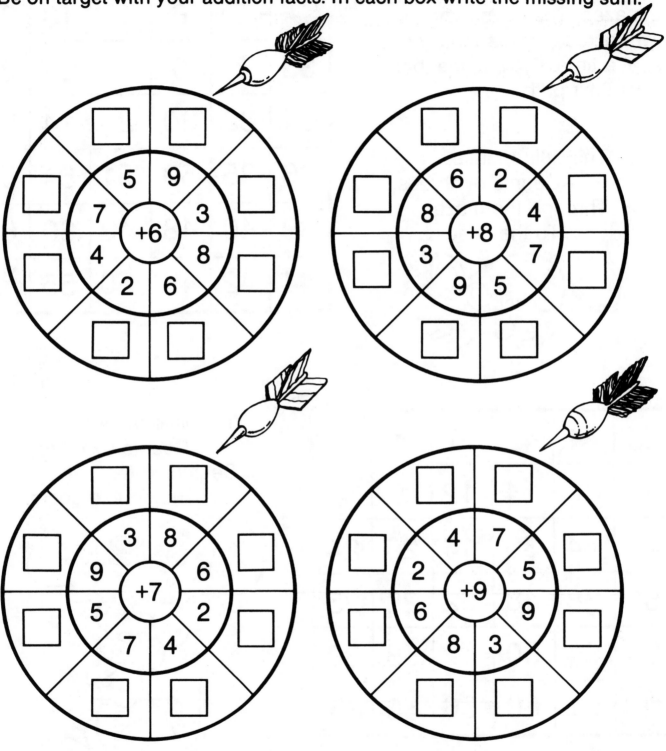

Try This! Create word problems for three of the addition facts above. Ask a friend to solve them.

Pots of Gold

Don't let the elf catch you not knowing which two numbers in the circle equal the sum on the top of each pot of gold. Draw a line to connect the two numbers needed.

A. 12
6
5   7
4

B. 16
5
8   8
7

C. 14
7
8   5
9

D. 13
3
7   5
8

E. 16
7
9   8
7

F. 17
9
9   8
7

G. 13
3
4   8
9

H. 11
6
7   3
5

I. 15
5
7   6
8

J. 18
6
9   9
7

K. 14
6
8   7
6

L. 11
8
4   7
5

M. 13
7
8   4
6

N. 9
4
7   5
6

O. 15
4
9   5
6

Try This! Draw a "pot of gold" in which all four numbers are needed to equal the sum.

 FS-32021 Math Activities

Topple the Bottles

To "topple" each set of bottles, subtract the number on the ball from
the number on each milk bottle.
Write the difference
on the bottle.

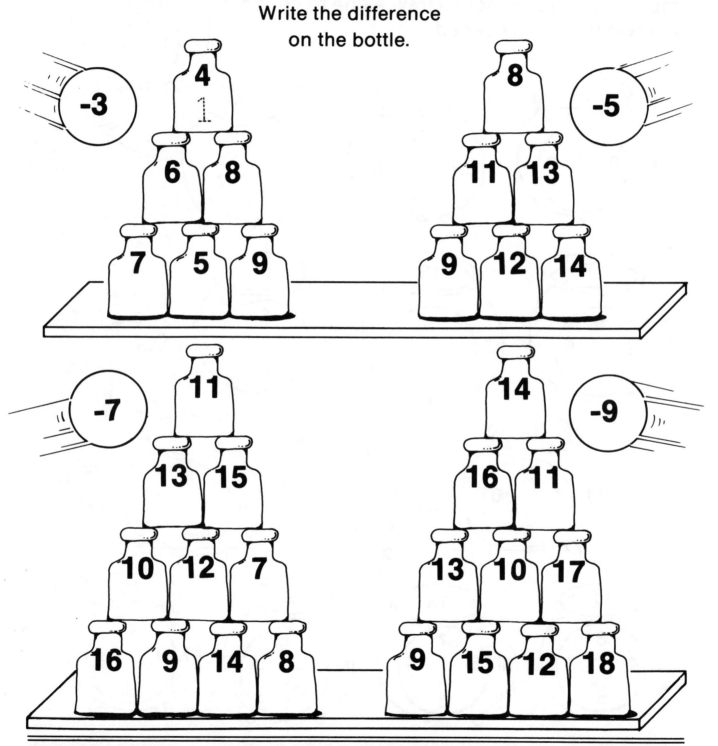

Try This! Draw a pyramid of milk bottles like the ones above for a friend to
"topple." Choose an even number to place in the ball.

38   FS-32021 Math Activities

Pick a Card

Don't be tricked as you pick your way through the Great
Zo's subtraction cards.

A.
11	9 ♠	13	12	15 ♣
−7	−4	−8	−8	−6

B.
16	13	18 ♦
−9	−4	−9

C.
12	11 ♣	15	13
−3	−4	−9	−5

D.
14 ♠	12	14	8 ♥
−8	−9	−6	−3

E.
15	13	16 ♣	12	14	11 ♠	12	14
−7	−6	−8	−6	−7	−5	−7	−9

F.
13	10 ♥	14	16	12	13	15	11 ♥
−7	−4	−5	−7	−5	−9	−8	−3

Try This! Follow these steps. Pick a number from 15 to 18. Subtract 9.
Add 5. Subtract 7. Add 4. Subtract 2. Add 9. What is your last answer?
Can you figure out the trick?

39   FS-32021 Math Activities

Name _____

What's It Worth?

1	2	3	4	5	6	1	2	3	4	5	6	1
a	b	c	d	e	f	g	h	i	j	k	l	m

2	3	4	5	6	1	2	3	4	5	6	1	2
n	o	p	q	r	s	t	u	v	w	x	y	z

Each letter above is worth from one to six points. Add the points for each letter to find out what a word is worth. Circle the correct answer.

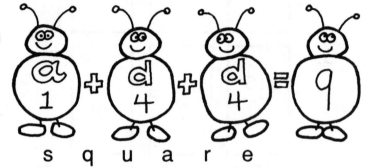

1. Which shape is worth more?

   c i r c l e   s q u a r e

   __ __ __ __ __ __ = ___   __ __ __ __ __ __ = ___

2. Which color is worth more?

   y e l l o w   o r a n g e

   __ __ __ __ __ __ = ___   __ __ __ __ __ __ = ___

3. Which fruit is worth more?

   b a n a n a   p e a c h

   __ __ __ __ __ __ = ___   __ __ __ __ __ = ___

4. Which bird is worth more?

   r o b i n   e a g l e

   __ __ __ __ __ = ___   __ __ __ __ __ = ___

5. Which object is worth more?

   p e n c i l   e r a s e r

   __ __ __ __ __ __ = ___   __ __ __ __ __ __ = ___

Brainwork! How many points is your full name worth?

Name

Stack o' Blocks

Add the numbers on each stack of blocks. Use the key to write a letter below each answer to find a message.

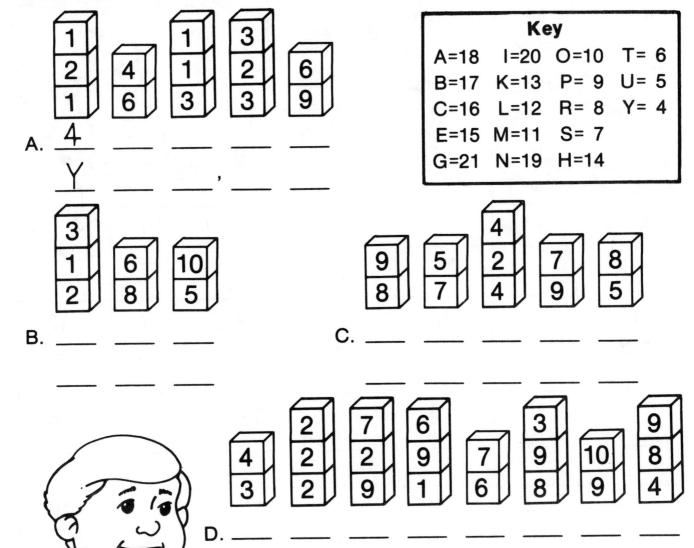

Key

A=18	I=20	O=10	T= 6
B=17	K=13	P= 9	U= 5
C=16	L=12	R= 8	Y= 4
E=15	M=11	S= 7	
G=21	N=19	H=14	

A. 4 __ __ __ __
   Y
   __ __ __ ,

B. __ __ __

C. __ __ __ __ __

D. __ __ __ __ __ __ __

E. __ __ __ __ __

Try This! Use a stack of blocks to create a coded message for a friend to solve. You may need to add letters to the key.

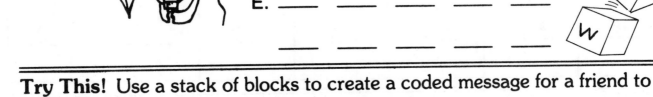

FS-32021 Math Activities

Subtraction Maze

Work each problem. To find a path to the end of the pie-eating contest, begin at START. Color all the boxes whose answers are even numbers.

	13 − 6	16 − 6	18 − 9			
	11 − 6	12 − 5	14 − 8	17 − 9	10 − 7	
13 − 4	12 − 9	15 − 8	7 − 4	12 − 4	16 − 7	13 − 8
11 − 8	16 − 9	10 − 4	13 − 7	11 − 5	14 − 9	8 − 3
14 − 7	12 − 3	12 − 8	15 − 6	10 − 9	9 − 2	10 − 3
17 − 8	15 − 7	13 − 5	11 − 4	9 − 4	12 − 7	8 − 5
START 14 − 6	11 − 7	14 − 5	9 − 6	10 − 5	7 − 2	11 − 2

Try This! Create a subtraction maze for a friend to solve.

Siz-z-zler Addition

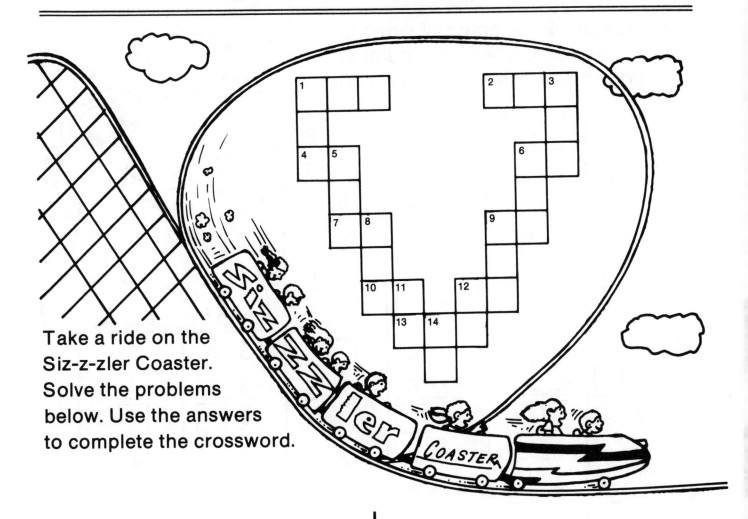

Take a ride on the Siz-z-zler Coaster. Solve the problems below. Use the answers to complete the crossword.

Across

1. 36
   +87

2. 72
   +29

4. 63
   +18

6. 8
   + 7

7. 27
   +34

9. 5
   + 9

10. 49
    +29

12. 16
    +66

13. 26
    +99

Down

1. 59
   +79

3. 79
   +26

5. 68
   +58

6. 98
   +46

8. 98
   +39

9. 64
   +78

11. 56
    +25

12. 36
    +49

14. 16
    + 6

Try This! Use the numbers 6, 7, 8, and 9 to make a two-digit addition problem that needs regrouping.

Addin' With Dragon

Mr. Dragon will be braggin' when you fill in each box with the number that correctly completes the problem.

A.
```
  4 6        □ 4        1 □        2 8
+ 2 □      + 5 7      + 7 7      + □ 9
-----      -----      -----      -----
  7 2        9 1        9 3        6 7
```

B.
```
  5 5        2 □        3 7        5 9
+ □ 9      + 6 5      + 1 9      + 2 9
-----      -----      -----      -----
  9 4        9 1        5 □        □ 8
```

C.
```
  2 5        5 7        1 8        □ 8        5 9        3 6
+ 4 □      + □ 7      + 7 6      + 2 6      + 3 8      + 4 6
-----      -----      -----      -----      -----      -----
  7 4        9 4        9 □        8 4        9 □        □ 2
```

D.
```
  2 8        1 7        2 6        3 9        2 7        4 4
+ □ 7      + □ 8      + 2 9      + 4 □      + □ 7      + 4 □
-----      -----      -----      -----      -----      -----
  6 5        7 5        5 □        8 5        8 4        9 2
```

E.
```
  3 9        1 5        6 □        □ 6        3 1        6 5
+ 2 4      + 4 8      + 1 6      + 3 7      + 4 □      + 2 5
-----      -----      -----      -----      -----      -----
  □ 3        6 □        8 3        6 3        8 0        9 □
```

F.
```
  1 9        2 □        2 9        3 8        2 □        5 6
+ □ 6      + 5 9      + 4 □      + 4 6      + 4 8      + □ 5
-----      -----      -----      -----      -----      -----
  5 5        8 6        7 8        □ 4        7 2        8 1
```

Try This! Complete the pattern: 2, 14, 26, ____, ____, ____ . Now create a different pattern for a friend to try.

FS-32021 Math Activities

Name _____

Slip-and-Slide Subtraction

Take a ride on the Slip-and-Slide. Solve each problem on your way.

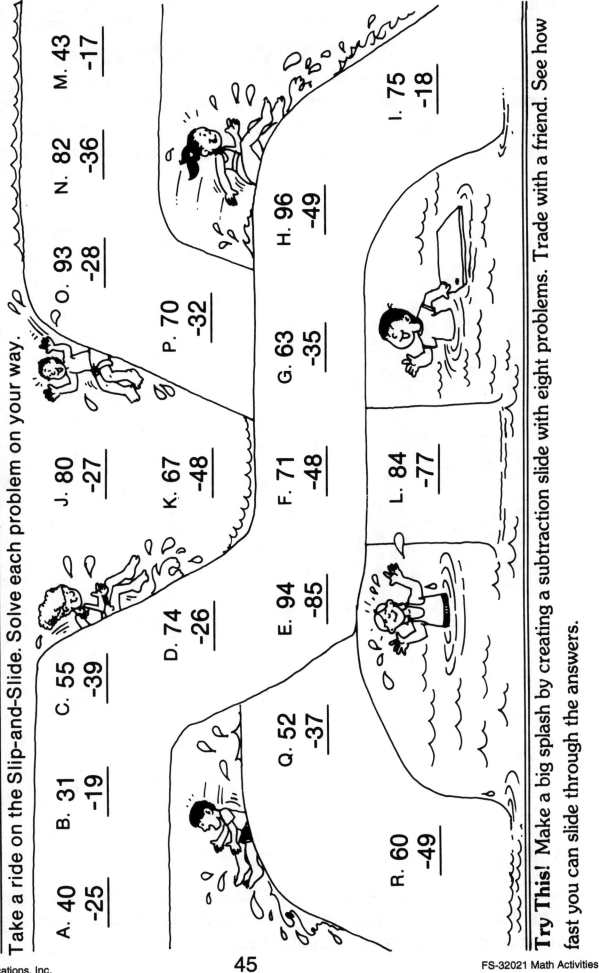

A. 40
−25

B. 31
−19

C. 55
−39

M. 43
−17

N. 82
−36

O. 93
−28

J. 80
−27

P. 70
−32

I. 75
−18

H. 96
−49

G. 63
−35

K. 67
−48

D. 74
−26

F. 71
−48

L. 84
−77

E. 94
−85

Q. 52
−37

R. 60
−49

Try This! Make a big splash by creating a subtraction slide with eight problems. Trade with a friend. See how fast you can slide through the answers.

Subtraction Action

Protect Subtraction Woman from the five evil crystals. You'll recognize them — they're the ones with the subtraction mistakes. Correct the answers and color the five evil crystals yellow.

Try This! Using these four digits (8, 2, 3, 5), create and solve two 2-digit subtraction problems that require regrouping.

FS-32021 Math Activities

Secret Code

Fill in each box with the number that solves the math sentence.

Add.   Subtract.

7 + 8 = [A]   14 − 8 = [O]

5 + 6 = [D]   17 − 9 = [R]

8 + [E] = 13   10 − [S] = 7

9 + [K] = 18   11 − [T] = 4

[M] + 10 = 10   [U] − 6 = 6

[N] + 8 = 12   [Y] − 4 = 9

Write the answer to the riddle.
Use the letters in the code boxes to help you.

What kinds of keys won't fit in your pocket?

___ ___ ___ ___ ___ ___ ___ ,
 11 6   4   9   5   13   3

___ ___ ___ ___ ___ ___ ___ ,
 0   6   4   9   5   13   3

___ ___ ___   ___ ___ ___ ___ ___ ___ ___
15 4 11   7 12 8   9   5 13   3

47

Name _____

Look Closely

Use the picture to work each problem below. Write the numbers on the lines. Write the addition or subtraction signs in the circles. Mark the final answer in the box.

1. Begin with the total number of children. Add the number of boys. Subtract the number of girls.

___ ◯ ___ ◯ ___ = ☐

2. Begin with the number of shoes. Subtract the number of children wearing pants. Add the number of children wearing shorts.

___ ◯ ___ ◯ ___ = ☐

3. Start with the number of shirts. Add the number of hats. Add the number of socks.

___ ◯ ___ ◯ ___ = ☐

4. Begin with the number of eyes you can see. Subtract the number of noses. Add the number of children wearing glasses.

___ ◯ ___ ◯ ___ = ☐

Brainwork! Color the picture. Then make up your own problem using the children in the picture.

Hocus, Pocus!

The wizard has created some gifts for you! First add, then subtract the two numbers in the stars on each gift. (Hint: Remember to place the larger number on top when you subtract.)

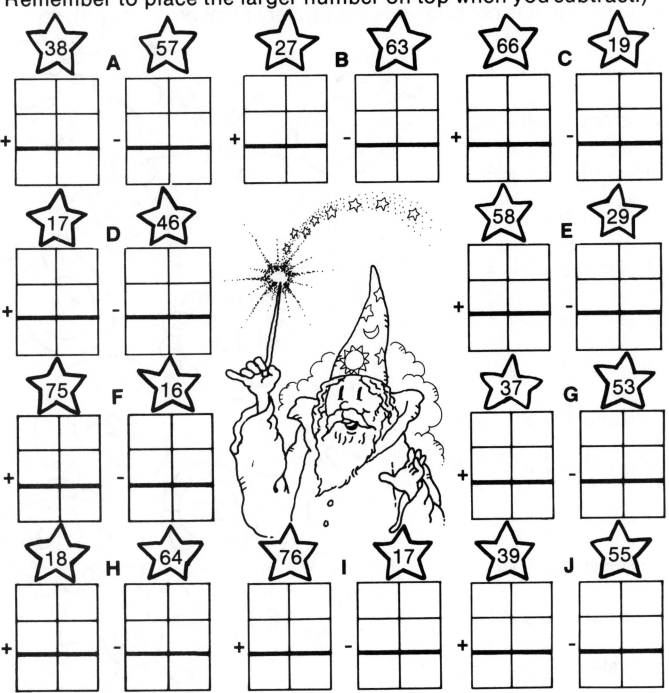

Try This! Pretend that you are the wizard and prepare a little "gift" for a classmate. Using the numbers 5, 6, 7, and 8, create two addition and two subtraction problems for a friend to solve.

FS-32021 Math Activities

The Mystery Number Game

To find the mystery number, first read each clue.
Then solve the addition problem in your head.
Color the circle with the answer after you solve it.
The number that is not colored is the mystery number.

1. It is not $7 + 3 + 5$.

2. It is not $4 + 8 + 10$.

3. It is not $6 + 9 + 4$.

4. It is not $9 + 1 + 6$.

5. It is not $2 + 7 + 4$.

6. It is not $5 + 1 + 8 + 3$.

7. It is not $4 + 7 + 0 + 3$.

8. It is not $8 + 3 + 2 + 7$.

9. It is not $9 + 4 + 3 + 2$.

10. It is not $3 + 5 + 6 + 9$.

11. It is not $6 + 10 + 4 + 5$.

12. It is not $5 + 3 + 3 + 10$.

The mystery number is _____ .

Brainwork! Color the petals of even-numbered flowers yellow. Color the petals of odd-numbered flowers orange.

FS-32021 Math Activities

Name the Robot

To find the robot's name:

• Read each clue.
• Solve the subtraction problem in your head.
• Color the space with the answer on the robot.

The number that is not colored is the robot's name.

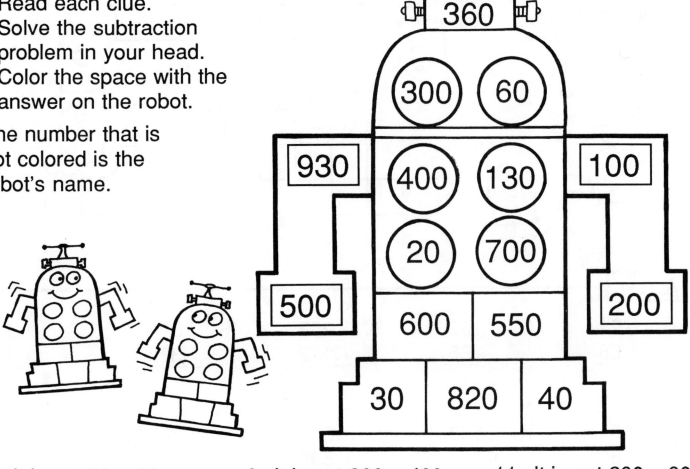

1. It is not 50 – 20.

2. It is not 70 – 10.

3. It is not 90 – 70.

4. It is not 80 – 40.

5. It is not 300 – 200.

6. It is not 900 – 400.

7. It is not 800 – 200.

8. It is not 600 – 300.

9. It is not 750 – 50.

10. It is not 460 – 60.

11. It is not 290 – 90.

12. It is not 140 – 10.

13. It is not 370 – 10.

14. It is not 580 – 30.

15. It is not 990 – 60.

The robot's name is _____ .

Brainwork! Write five subtraction problems you could solve in your head. Use the number 760 in each problem.

Cross Number Critters

Solve the addition
and subtraction
problems below.
Use the answers
to complete the
cross number
puzzle.

Across

A.	124 + 68	C.	156 + 86	D.	257 + 182	F.	529 + 328	G.	176 + 165
I.	455 + 266	K.	133 + 387	L.	308 + 598	N.	342 + 295	O.	254 + 46

Down

B.	51 − 27	C.	284 − 257	E.	128 − 35	F.	715 − 634	H.	551 − 149
I.	550 − 480	J.	70 − 51	K.	60 − 3	M.	753 − 690		

Brainwork! Use the digits 3, 4, 6, 7, and 8 to make a subtraction problem.

Fact Search

Fly through the heavens and circle the hidden multiplication sentences. Add an **x** sign and an =sign.

A.	1	(0 × 2 = 0)		1
B.	3	1	3	2	5
C.	2	2	7	14	2
D.	1	4	8	2	16
E.	0	5	0	3	3
F.	12	6	2	12	6
G.	1	0	1	1	1
H.	10	5	2	10	12
I.	1	9	0	9	0
J.	9	2	18	6	2

K.	14	7	7	1	7
L.	2	5	0	10	0
M.	2	4	8	4	12
N.	4	2	2	4	6
O.	0	1	5	1	5
P.	4	0	0	2	4
Q.	2	11	2	11	22
R.	8	1	9	9	18
S.	6	1	6	2	8
T.	7	7	0	0	7
U.	3	2	6	3	3
V.	7	1	8	1	8
W.	12	2	24	2	6
X.	8	0	0	4	2
Y.	6	1	2	2	12
Z.	10	2	20	10	1

Try This! Make a fact-search puzzle using the multiplication facts for 5.

FS-32021 Math Activities

Multiplication Puzzle

Fix this mixed-up puzzle. First cut out the puzzle pieces. Then put the puzzle together by matching each multiplication problem with its correct answer. Glue the finished puzzle on another sheet of paper.

Example:

3 x 5 = | 15

5 x 4 = 6 x 3 =	7 x 3 = 7 x 4 = 18	28 3 x 2 =
20 8 x 4 = 9 x 4 =	36 21 8 x 5 = 3 x 5 =	15 6 9 x 3 =
32 2 x 4 =	8 7 x 2 = 40	14 27

FS-32021 Math Activities

Munch a Bunch

Munch through these super subs. Fill in each  with the number that makes the number sentence true.

A. $4 \times 8 =$ ◯

B. ◯ $\times 5 = 45$

C. $3 \times$ ◯ $= 21$

D. $5 \times 6 =$ ◯

E. $2 \times$ ◯ $= 18$

F. ◯ $\times 7 = 35$

G. $4 \times$ ◯ $= 16$

H. $5 \times 5 =$ ◯

I. ◯ $\times 8 = 24$

J. $4 \times$ ◯ $= 36$

K. $8 \times 5 =$ ◯

L. $4 \times$ ◯ $= 28$

M. ◯ $\times 9 = 27$

N. $5 \times$ ◯ $= 20$

O. $4 \times 6 =$ ◯

Try This! Use the numbers (16, 2, 8), (6, 18, 3) and (4, 24, 6) to create three multiplication number sentences for a friend to solve.

FS-32021 Math Activities

King Midas's Favorites

King Midas loves number words. Turn his multiplication crossword into a puzzle filled with some of his favorites.

Across

1. 3 x ____ = 24
3. ____ x 4 = 24
5. ____ x 5 = 40
6. 3 x ____ = 21
7. 5 x ____ = 45
9. 4 x ____ = 40
11. 5 x ____ = 25
13. ____ x 3 = 15
14. 3 x ____ = 27

Down

1. 4 x ____ = 32
2. ____ x 4 = 12
3. 5 x ____ = 35
4. ____ x 4 = 28
8. 3 x ____ = 33
9. ____ x 6 = 18
10. 4 x ____ = 36
11. 4 x ____ = 16
12. ____ x 6 = 30

Word Box

three
four
five
six
seven
eight
nine
ten
eleven

Try This! Write a story problem which can be solved with one of the multiplication facts from the puzzle.

56   FS-32021 Math Activities

Name_____

Multiplication Secret Code

Fill in each box with the
number that solves the
multiplication math sentence.

2 x 5 = ☐A

4 x ☐B = 16

3 x 9 = ☐C

☐E x 5 = 30

7 x 4 = ☐G

3 x ☐H = 0

9 x 2 = ☐I

☐L x 4 = 12

5 x ☐M = 35

8 x 3 = ☐N

7 x ☐O = 56

4 x 5 = ☐P

9 x ☐R = 81

☐S x 7 = 35

5 x 5 = ☐T

8 x ☐U = 8

☐W x 6 = 12

6 x 6 = ☐Y

Use the code to solve these riddles. Write the letter from the box that
matches the numbers.

1. What has a tongue but cannot talk?

___ ___ ___ ___ ___
10   5   0   8   6

2. What has feathers but does not squawk?

___ ___ ___ ___ ___ ___ ___
10   20 18   3   3   8   2

3. What has legs but cannot walk?

___ ___ ___ ___ ___ ___ ___   ___ ___ ___ ___ ___
10   25 10   4   3   6   8   9   27   0   10 18   9

Brainwork! Write three multiplication problems whose answer is 12.

A Day at the Park

Use this picture to work each problem below. Write numbers on the lines. Write the addition, subtraction, or multiplication signs in the circles. Then mark the final answer in the box.

1. Begin with the total number of children. Multiply by the number of boys. Subtract the number of girls.

___ ◯ ___ = ___
___ ◯ ___ = ☐

2. Begin with the number of flowers. Subtract the number of children. Multiply by the number of trees.

___ ◯ ___ = ___
___ ◯ ___ = ☐

3. Begin with the number of bicycles. Add the number of park benches. Multiply by the number of swings.

___ ◯ ___ = ___
___ ◯ ___ = ☐

4. Begin with the number of dogs. Add the number of birds. Multiply by the number of cats.

___ ◯ ___ = ___
___ ◯ ___ = ☐

Brainwork! Write your own math problem using objects from the picture.

 FS-32021 Math Activities

Mr. Magician's Hat Tricks

This array of X's shows these facts.

X X X   4 x 3 = 12
X X X   3 x 4 = 12
X X X   12 ÷ 4 = 3
X X X   12 ÷ 3 = 4

Write **two multiplication facts** and **two division facts** shown by the things Mr. Magician has pulled out of his hat.

1. _____

_____

_____

2.  _____

_____

_____

3. _____

_____

_____

4. ????? _____
?????
????? _____

_____

_____

5. 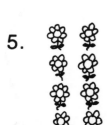 _____

_____

_____

6. _____

_____

_____

_____

7. !!!!!!!!! _____
!!!!!!!!!
_____

_____

8.  _____

_____

_____

_____

9. _____

_____

_____

Try This! Solve this problem. Then create a problem for a friend to do.

3 ⟶ x 4 ⟶ ÷ 2 ⟶ x 5 = ____

Circus Segments

A straight line drawn between two points is called a **segment**.
Use a ruler to draw each segment. Then color the picture.

1. segment AB ($\overline{AB}$)
2. segment BC ($\overline{BC}$)
3. segment CD ($\overline{CD}$)
4. segment DE ($\overline{DE}$)
5. segment FJ ($\overline{FJ}$)
6. segment GK ($\overline{GK}$)
7. segment HL ($\overline{HL}$)
8. segment IM ($\overline{IM}$)
9. segment NR ($\overline{NR}$)
10. segment OS ($\overline{OS}$)
11. segment PT ($\overline{PT}$)
12. segment QU ($\overline{QU}$)
13. segment VW ($\overline{VW}$)
14. segment XY ($\overline{XY}$)
15. segment VY ($\overline{VY}$)
16. segment XW ($\overline{XW}$)

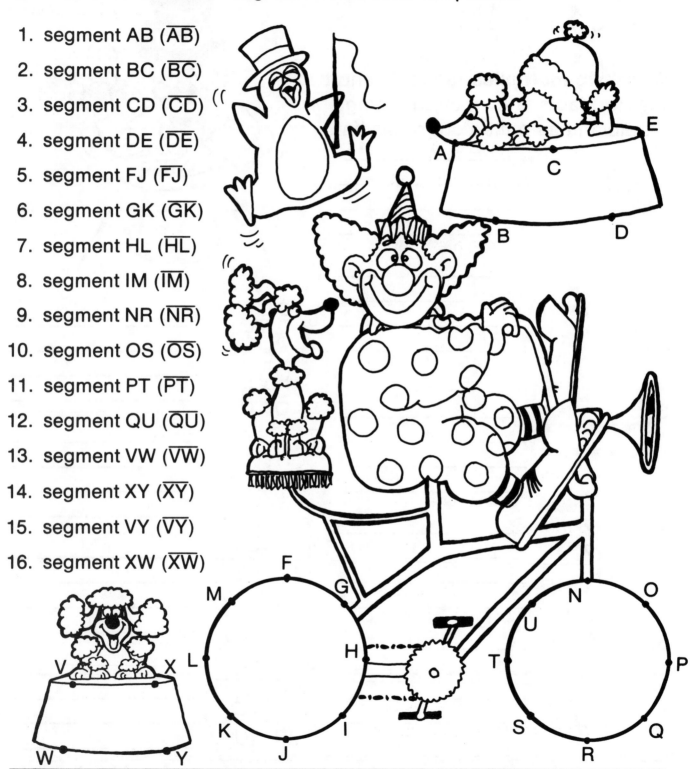

Try This! Draw your own circus picture using at least four segments.

FS-32021 Math Activities

Corners and Sides

Triangles have three sides and three corners.

A • shows each corner.

An **X** marks each side.

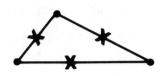

Write the letter of the shape that answers each riddle. Then label each shape with its name.

Shape Name

_____ 1. I have three straight sides and the same number of corners. I am a **triangle.**

A

A. _____

_____ 2. I have four straight sides all the same length. I have four corners. I am a **square**.

B

B. _____

_____ 3. I have four straight sides. I have four square corners. I am a **rectangle**.

C

C. _____

_____ 4. I have five corners and five straight sides. I am a **pentagon**.

D

D. _____

_____ 5. I have six corners and six straight sides. I am a **hexagon**.

E

E. _____

_____ 6. I have no straight sides and no corners. I am a **circle**.

F

F. _____

Try This! Draw a shape that has ten corners and ten sides.

Geometric Dinosaurs

Brighten up these dinosaurs!
Color all triangles (△) green.
Color all rectangles (▭) purple.
Color all circles (○) blue.
Color the remaining parts brown.

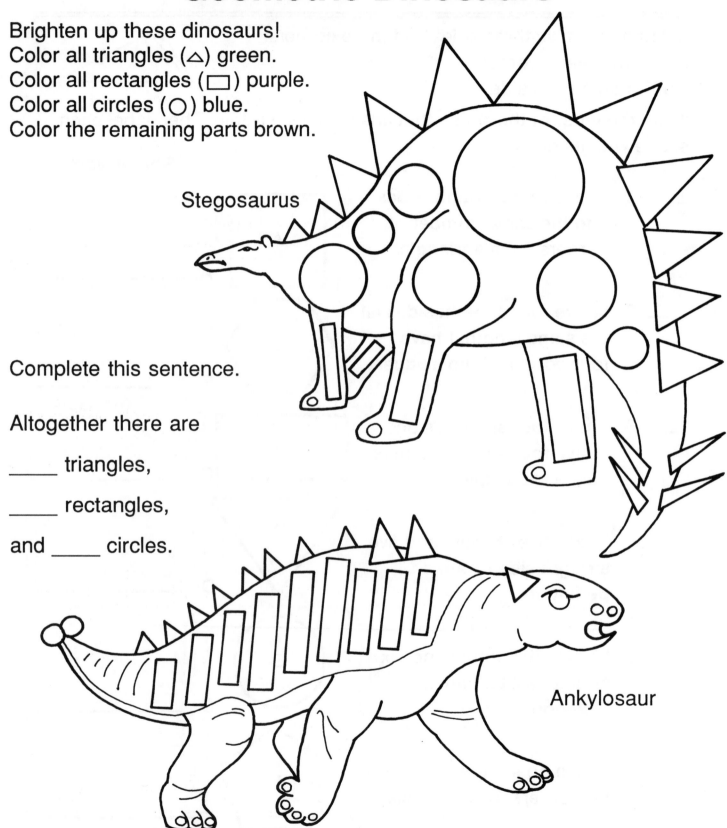

Stegosaurus

Complete this sentence.

Altogether there are

____ triangles,

____ rectangles,

and ____ circles.

Ankylosaur

Brainwork! Draw a picture using triangles, rectangles, and circles.

     FS-32021 Math Activities

Sorting Shapes

Look at these shapes.

Write the numbers of all the shapes that would belong in each bag.

A.
2
5
8
circles

B.
triangles

C.
squares

D.
rectangles,
not squares

E.
unshaded
shapes

F.
shaded
shapes

G.
not circles

H.
not triangles

I.
not squares

Try This! Draw and label a bag in which shapes 1, 3, 4, 6, 7, 9, 10, 11 and 12 could fit.

63

FS-32021 Math Activities

Same Shapes

Cut out and arrange the pieces on the grid so:

• each piece shares a side with another piece that has the same shape

• each column (down) has more than two different shapes.

Glue the pieces in place.

FS-32021 Math Activities

Breakfast at the Waffle Hopper

Everyone ordered toppings for their waffles. Find out how much each person's breakfast cost.

a. Jim put strawberries and whipped cream on his waffle.
Cost: _____

b. Mary Ellen put lots of butter on her waffle. Then she put a scoop of ice cream on top.
Cost: _____

c. Chris loves sweets. She put a big mountain of chocolate chips and cherries on her waffle.
Cost: _____

d. Carlos and Rich decided to share a waffle. Carlos wanted whipped cream on his half. Rich put chocolate chips on his half.
Cost: _____

e. Ray was very hungry. He put ice cream and strawberries on his waffle but that wasn't enough. He added a pile of whipped cream.
Cost: _____

f. Phil likes fruit. He covered his waffle with cherries and strawberries. Then he put a spoonful of chocolate chips on top.
Cost: _____

Lunch Specials

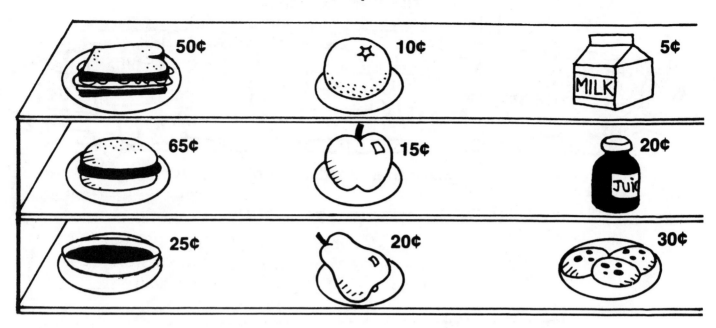

Find out how much each person's lunch cost.

a. Jean bought a hamburger and a bottle of juice.

Cost: _____

b. Marty decided that the sandwich looked good so he put it on his tray. He bought a pear too.

Cost: _____

c. Sherry was very cold. She picked out a bowl of soup and an orange.

Cost: _____

d. Maureen ordered a hamburger and a carton of milk.

Cost: _____

e. Chuck bought cookies and an orange. Then he put a carton of milk on his tray.

Cost: _____

f. Phil likes fruit. He picked out a pear, an orange and cookies for his lunch.

Cost: _____

Bonus: Chuck has 85¢. How much change does he get back?

_____

Bonus: Phil has 30¢. Does he have enough money? _____ What food should he put back? _____

The Birthday Party

a. Marie bought 3 balloons. They cost 15¢ each.
Total cost: _____

b. Leslie bought 2 plates at 25¢ each. She also bought a 10¢ blower.
Total cost: _____

c. Father bought cake and candles. The cake cost 65¢. The candles were 25¢.
Total cost: _____

d. Buy 4 cups. Each one costs 15¢. Then buy a can of juice. It costs 40¢.
Total cost: _____

e. The party hats cost 35¢ each. Buy 2. Then buy a game for 25¢.
Total cost: _____

f. Everyone wants a prize. Buy 3 toys for 25¢ each. A big box to put them in costs 15¢.
Total cost: _____

g. You are going to play a game. Buy 4 blindfolds and 2 paper elephants. The blindfolds cost 10¢ each. The elephants cost 25¢ each.
Total cost: _____

Bonus:
How much more expensive are the party things in balloon d. compared to balloon c.? _____

Name _____

Easter Baskets

Find the cost of each person's basket of eggs.

a.

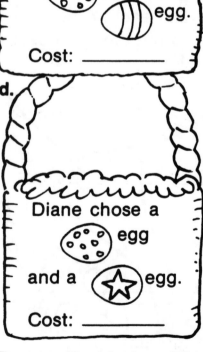

Michelle bought a ⬭ egg and a ⬭ egg.

Cost: _____

b.

Peter bought a ♡ egg and a ⚡ egg.

Cost: _____

c.

Anthony picked out a ☆ egg and a ⬭ egg.

Cost: _____

d.

Diane chose a ⬭ egg and a ☆ egg.

Cost: _____

e.

Nicole's favorite eggs are: ⬭, ♡ and ☆

Cost: _____

f.

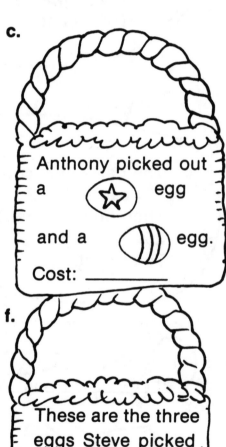

These are the three eggs Steve picked out: ⬭, ⬭, ⬭

Cost: _____

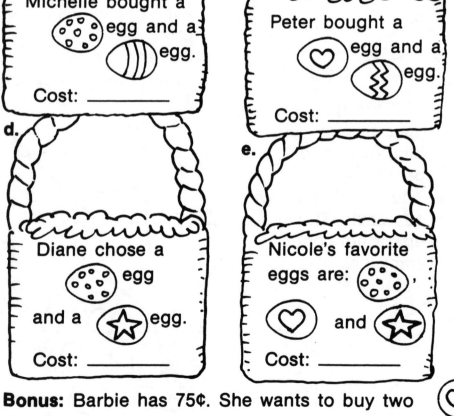

Bonus: Barbie has 75¢. She wants to buy two ♡ eggs and a ⚡ egg. Can she buy them? _____ Tell why or why not.

FS-32021 Math Activities

Name _____

The Elves' New Clothes

All the  are going out to buy their winter clothes. Find out how much money each  has left after he shops.

a. Sweezy bought a new pair of . He had 30¢.

Change: _____

b. Bopey needs a 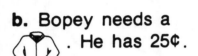. He has 25¢.

Change: _____

c. Toc has 65¢. He wants to buy a pair of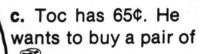

Change: _____

d. Sloopy will buy a pair of 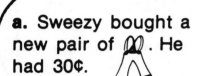. He has 25¢.

Change: _____

e. Frumpy's is all worn out. He needs a new one. Frumpy has 50¢.

Change: _____

f. Hoppy is going to buy 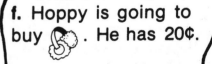. He has 20¢.

Change: _____

Bonus: Toc wants to buy a and a pair of  . How much do

they cost? _____ How much change will he get back from 70¢? _____

69

A Penny Saved

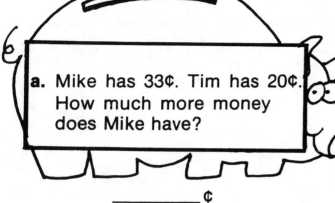

a. Mike has 33¢. Tim has 20¢. How much more money does Mike have?

_____ ¢

b. Nancy had 45¢. She gave 34¢ to Sue. How much does Nancy have left?

_____ ¢

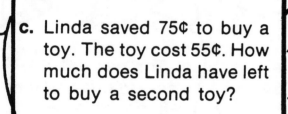

c. Linda saved 75¢ to buy a toy. The toy cost 55¢. How much does Linda have left to buy a second toy?

_____ ¢

d. Bill has earned 30¢. He wants to buy something that costs 62¢. How much more does he need to earn?

_____ ¢

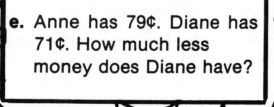

e. Anne has 79¢. Diane has 71¢. How much less money does Diane have?

_____ ¢

f. A teddy bear costs 86¢. A toy train costs 53¢. What is the difference in price between the two toys?

_____ ¢

Bonus: A whistle costs 41¢. A balloon costs 45¢. Will Anne (in bank **e.**) be able to buy both toys? _____ If not, how much more money will she need? _____

FS-32021 Math Activities

How Much?

a. John earned 73¢ raking lawns. He earned 18¢ sweeping the porch. How much did he earn all together? _____

b. Jan is going to baby-sit for two days. She will earn 55¢ the first day and 36¢ the second day. How much will Jan earn all together?

_____

c. Karen is going to buy a piece of chocolate cake for herself. It costs 43¢. She will buy two cookies for her friend. They cost 19¢ each. How much will Karen spend? _____

d. For getting two A's on his report card, Jeff's dad gave him 65¢. He got three B's too so Dad gave him 35¢. How much did Jeff have all together? _____

e. I want to buy a toy whistle. The one I want costs 49¢. How much will two cost?

_____

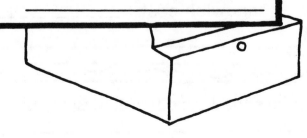

f. Let's go to the movies. A ticket costs 75¢. A bag of popcorn costs 15¢. How much will it cost to go to the movies? _____

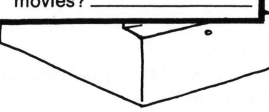

FS-32021 Math Activities

Name _____

Sandwich Sampler

How do you find out?
1) Ellen bought 3 apples. Each one cost 15¢.
2) She also bought 2 pears. Each one cost 10¢.
3) What is the total cost?

1.
15¢
15¢
15¢
___
45¢

2.
10¢
10¢
___
20¢

3.
45¢
20¢
___
Total: 65¢

Work these problems following the example above.

a. Kelly wants 2 slices of turkey and 3 slices of cheese. (a) The turkey costs 20¢ a slice. (b) The cheese is 10¢ a slice. (c) What is the total cost? _____

b. How much will (a) 4 olives at 5¢ each and (b) 3 tomatoes at 2¢ each cost? _____

c. I want a slice of ham. (a) It costs 48¢. (b) I also want 3 tomatoes. They cost 13¢ each. (c) What will everything cost? _____

d. Lynn made a big sandwich. (a) She chose 2 slices of chicken first. Each slice cost 20¢. (b) Then she picked out 3 slices of cheese. Each slice cost 12¢. (c) Last she put 2 pieces of bacon on top. Bacon costs 10¢ a piece. Her sandwich cost: _____

Bonus: A bowl of soup costs 45¢. Buy 2. A ham sandwich costs 30¢. Buy 3. Which food costs more? _____

FS-32021 Math Activities

Stuffed Pet Sale

Read each problem.

1. Write the regular price under each animal.
2. Write the sale price on the tag.
3. Solve the problems.

a.

The dog is **on sale** for 54¢. Last week it cost 84¢. How much less does the dog cost on sale? _____

b.

The mouse used to cost 45¢. Now it's **on sale** for 32¢. What is the difference in price?

_____

c.

The cat is **on sale** for 68¢. It used to cost 80¢. How much less does it cost now? _____

d.

This is such a cute turtle. It costs 77¢ **on sale**. It used to cost 90¢. How much less does it cost now?

_____

e.

Last week, the bird cost 69¢. Now it is **on sale** for 40¢. How much money was taken off the regular price?

_____

f.

This fish does not need water. Last week, it cost 36¢. This week it is **on sale** for only 25¢. Was more than 5¢ taken off? _____ How much more? _____

Bonus: You have 50¢. How much more money will you need to buy the cat? _____

FS-32021 Math Activities

Tara's Treasure Chest

 89¢
 58¢
 86¢
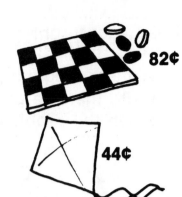 82¢

 75¢
 38¢
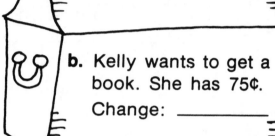 63¢ 44¢

Six girls have been invited to Ellen's birthday party. They are all going to buy presents. Find out how much change each girl will get.

a. Ann has 90¢. She is going to buy a game.
Change: _____

b. Kelly wants to get a book. She has 75¢.
Change: _____

c. Chris chose the stuffed dog. She has 95¢.
Change: _____

d. Jenny has 81¢. She will buy paints and a brush.
Change: _____

e. Nicole has 57¢. She wants to buy the purse. Can she do it? _____
How much more money does she need? _____

f. Kim's favorite toy is the kite. She has saved 38¢. Can she buy it? _____
How much money does she need to borrow? _____

Bonus: Kelly has changed her mind. She wants to buy 2 jump ropes. Can she buy them? Tell why or why not. _____

FS-32021 Math Activities

Name _____

Paco's Pizza Palace

Pizza Slice		Spaghetti		Drinks	
Cheese	30¢	1 meatball	25¢	Milk	20¢
Ham	35¢	2 meatballs	30¢	Cola	15¢
Sausage	40¢	3 meatballs	40¢	Root beer	30¢

a. Dan bought a slice of ham pizza and a carton of milk.

Cost: _____

b. Marilyn had 95¢. She bought spaghetti with 2 meatballs. What was her change?

Change: _____

c. Jim wants a slice of sausage pizza, spaghetti with 1 meatball and root beer. How much money does he need?

Cost: _____

d. Barbara is going to buy two slices of cheese pizza and two colas.

Cost: _____

e. Tony has 85¢. He wants to buy spaghetti with 3 meatballs, a slice of cheese pizza and a carton of milk. Does he have enough money? _____ How much more does he need? _____

Bonus: Gina has 70¢. Write two things she can buy with all her money.

_____

1. Steve has .40 He bought a toy football for .30. How much money did he get back?

2. Michael earned .80. He gave his brother .50. How much did Michael have left?

1.

3. Ellen wants to buy a .35 ice cream cone. She only has .15. How much more money does she need?

2.

3.

4. Dad gave Tim $1.00. Tim put half the money in the bank. How much did Tim keep?

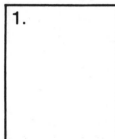

5. A new watch costs $1.85. Randy has .75. How much more money does Randy need to save?

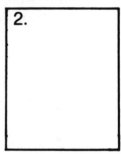

4.

5.

6. A newspaper costs .20. Barbie gave the man .90. What change did she get back?

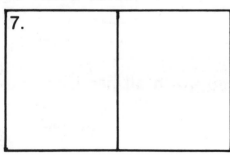

6.

8. Chris bought a sandwich for .90. She bought an orange for .25. Chris gave the man $1.15. How much did lunch cost? How much change did Chris get?

7. John has .65. He bought two apples. They cost .15 each. How much did John spend? How much did he have left?

7. |

8. |

FS-32021 Math Activities

Circus Time

Everybody in the circus is hungry. They all want to eat something before the show starts.

a. Albert bought peanuts and a soft drink.
Cost: _____

b. Diane loves candied apples. She paid 35¢. What was her change?
_____

c. Pete had an ice cream cone and popcorn.
Cost: _____

d. Judy was very hungry. She ate a hot dog and ice cream.
Cost: _____

e. Edgar bought cotton candy. He paid the man 45¢. How much change did Edgar get back?
_____

Bonus: Judy bought peanuts, a soft drink and a hot dog for her brother. How much did it all cost? _____ Judy gave the man $1.00. Did she get any change back? _____ If so, how much? _____

77

seventy-five cents

fifty cents

twenty-five cents

fifteen cents

Cents are often shown with a cents sign (¢) or with a decimal point ($.50). When you have more than a dollar, use a decimal point ($1.55 not 155¢).

Example: Sue has one dollar and twenty-five cents. She wants to buy a 🥧 . It costs fifteen cents.

```
  1.25
- .15
-------
$1.10
```

Write the problems. Find the change. (Don't forget the decimal points!)

1. A 💍 costs two dollars and fifty cents. Patrick has one dollar and fifty cents. Subtract to find out how much more money Patrick needs.

```
-
____
```

2. A 🥤 costs one dollar and forty-five cents. 🍦 is one dollar and twenty cents. Add to find out how much both foods cost.

```
+
____
```

3. Lou earned two dollars and ten cents. His father gave him one dollar and twenty-five cents. How much did Lou have altogether?

```
+
____
```

4. Kelly had three dollars and seventy-five cents. She lost one dollar and fifty cents. How much did she have left?

```
-
____
```

5. Sam's new 🐴 needs a 🪑 . The saddle costs four dollars and thirty cents. Sam has four dollars and fifteen cents. Can he buy the saddle? _____ Tell why or why not. _____

FS-32021 Math Activities

Name _____

How much money did everyone have before they bought ice cream?

Vanilla   55¢

Mint   20¢

Cherry   35¢

Chocolate   40¢

Banana   30¢

Orange   65¢

1. Mark bought a scoop of banana. His change: .20

2. Sue bought a scoop of mint. Her change: .65

3. Pete bought 1 scoop of cherry and 1 scoop of chocolate. His change: .75

4. Donna bought a scoop of orange. Her change: .45

5. David bought 2 scoops of vanilla. His change: .25

Linda bought 1 scoop of orange, mint and banana. Her change: .35

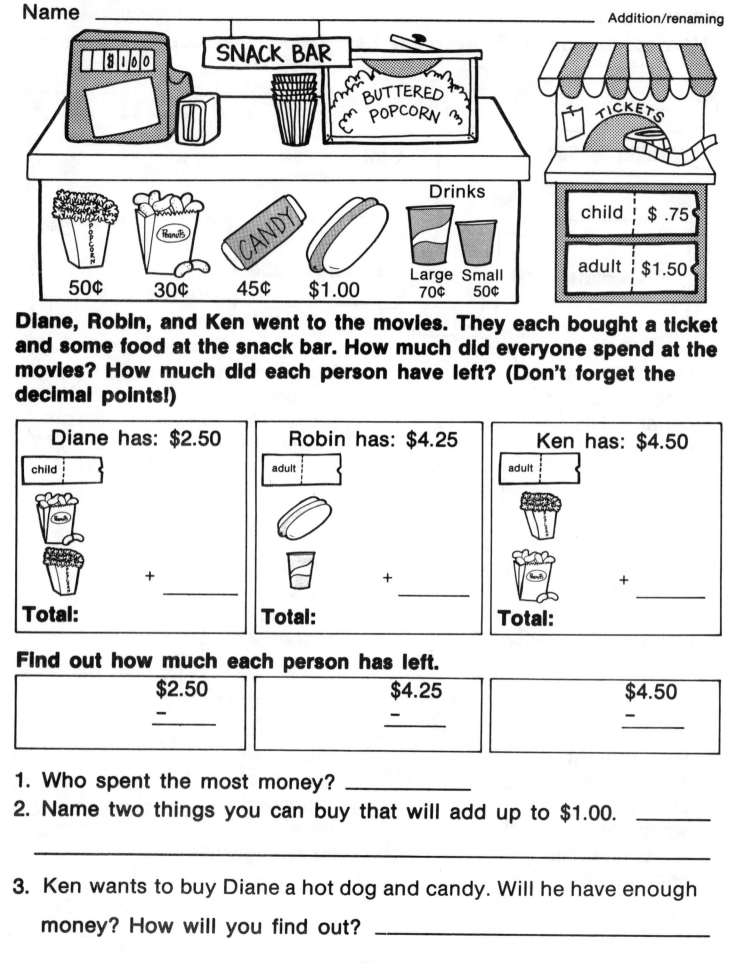

SNACK BAR

BUTTERED POPCORN

Drinks

50¢   30¢   45¢ $1.00   Large Small
                                70¢   50¢

TICKETS

| child | $ .75 |
| adult | $1.50 |

Diane, Robin, and Ken went to the movies. They each bought a ticket and some food at the snack bar. How much did everyone spend at the movies? How much did each person have left? (Don't forget the decimal points!)

Diane has: $2.50

child

_____ + _____

Total:

Robin has: $4.25

adult

_____ + _____

Total:

Ken has: $4.50

adult

_____ + _____

Total:

Find out how much each person has left.

$2.50
−_____

$4.25
−_____

$4.50
−_____

1. Who spent the most money? _____

2. Name two things you can buy that will add up to $1.00. _____

_____

3. Ken wants to buy Diane a hot dog and candy. Will he have enough

money? How will you find out? _____

How much did each girl spend on food? How much change was left?

Kate bought peanuts and popcorn.		Peggy went to the magic show! Later, she got a soda.		Sharon took a pony ride and ate some cookies.	
Add	Subtract	Add	Subtract	Add	Subtract

Tina bought a soda, cookies and went to the magic show.		**1.** Who has the most money left over? _____
Add	Subtract	**2.** Name two things Peggy could buy with her change. _____
		3. Can Kate go to the magic show? _____ Tell why or why not. _____ _____

Write the number sentence and label your answer.

1. John saved $5.95. If he buys the Rainbow Game, how much will he have left?

$$5.95 - 3.80 = 2.15$$

John will have ____ $2.15 ____ left.

2. If Ann gives the sales person $5.49 to pay for the race car, how much money will she get back?

_____

Ann will get _____ back.

3. Tammy wanted to buy the walkie-talkies. Her dad gave her $9.87. How much money will be left over?

_____

There will be _____ left.

4. If Jim had $9.68 and he bought a Frisbee, how much money would he have then?

_____

Jim would have _____ .

5. Mark has $5.69. If he buys a race car, how much will he still have?

_____

Mark will still have _____ .

6. If Jan had $9.85 and bought the Rainbow Game, how much would she have left?

_____

Jan would have _____ left.

FS-32021 Math Activities

Name _____

Write the number sentence and label your answer.

1. Mike had $6.91. He bought a shirt. How much did he have left?

$$6.91 - 5.87 = 1.04$$

Mike had _____ $1.04 _____ left.

2. Linda bought the skirt. If she gave the sales person $9.70, how much change did she get?

_____

Linda got _____ change.

3. Jim's dad gave him $9.25. If Jim bought the pants, how much money will his dad get back?

_____

He will get back _____ .

4. Mark bought the boy's hat. If he started with $4.50, how much does he have left?

_____

Mark had _____ left.

5. Ann's mother had $9.79. If Ann buys the blouse, how much change will her mother get?

_____

She will get _____ change.

6. If Nancy buys the girl's hat, how much change will she get from a $5.00 bill?

_____

Nancy will get _____ change.

Name _____

Write the number sentence and label your answer.

1. Andy made $2.75 on Saturday and $3.25 on Sunday. How much did he make altogether?

_____

Andy made _____ .

2. Mike saved $7.82. He spent $4.95 on a gift for his brother. How much did he have left?

_____

Mike had _____ left.

3. Susan spent $6.84 on a gift for her mother and $1.77 to get it wrapped. How much did she spend in all?

_____

Susan spent _____ in all.

4. Bob bought 3 toys. One was $1.49, another was $2.37, and the third was $.38. What was the total?

_____

Total cost was _____ .

5. Mary had $9.00. She paid $2.64 for her sister's birthday gift. How much did she have then?

_____

Mary had _____ then.

6. Jack saved $3.49. On the way to the store, he lost $.27. How much can he spend now?

_____

Jack can spend _____ now.

7. If Linda started with $8.70 and spent $1.57 on her baby sister, how much money does she have left?

_____

Linda has _____ left.

FS-32021 Math Activities

Vito's Sporting Goods is having a sale on football equipment. The original price is on the item. The sale price is on the tag.

Vito's Sporting Goods

Mark bought 2 footballs. (a) How much did they cost? _____ (b) How much did Mark save? _____

	Add			**Add**		**Subtract**
(a) Sale	4.25		(b) Regular	5.95	Total regular price	11.90
price	4.25		price	5.95	Total sale price	− 8.50
	$8.50			**$11.90**	Mark saved:	**$3.40**

a. Coach Benson bought 3 pairs of shoes. How much did the shoes cost? _____ How much money did he save? _____

c. Our team wants to buy 3 helmets. How much will they cost? _____ How much will the team save? _____

Bonus: The team has $40.00. After buying the helmets, how much change did they have? _____ Name two other items the team can buy with their change.

_____

_____

b. Pam and Patty are twins. Pam bought 2 shirts. Patty bought 2 helmets. How much did Pam spend? _____ How much did Patty spend? _____ How much did Pam save? _____ How much did Patty save? _____

d. Dad bought me 3 footballs. How much did he spend? _____ How much did he save? _____

Skills: 3-digit addition,
Subtraction, Regrouping

Morry's Shoe Sale

a. I am going to the beach this summer. Three pairs of flip-flops would be great! How much will they cost?

_____

b. Tom wants to buy a pair of Martian shoes. His mother will give him $8.50. How much money will Tom have to add?

_____

c. Kerri will buy 2 pairs of boots. How much money will she save when she buys them on sale? _____

d. Find out which pair of shoes was reduced more in price-- the saddle shoes or the boots.

_____

e. Mom bought 2 pairs of Martian shoes. How much did she save when she bought them on sale? _____

Bonus: Scott bought a pair of boots at another store for $12.95. How much would he have saved if he had bought them at Morry's? _____

FS-32021 Math Activities

Name _____

Trick or Treat

It's Halloween! Six children went to the party store to pick
out their costumes. Find out how much each child spent.
Find out how much change each person got back.

a. Sam.....

bought a mask and
a cape. He had $7.00.

Spent: Change:

_____   _____

c. Robin.....

bought rabbit ears
and teeth. She had
$5.50.

Spent: Change:

_____   _____

b. Susan.....

bought wings and
a crown. She had
$4.25.

Spent: Change:

_____   _____

d. Matt.....

bought a mask, a
halo and shoes.
He had $5.75.

Spent: Change:

_____   _____

Bonus: Who has enough change to buy a mask and a

halo? _____

87   FS-32021 Math Activities

Name _____

On Monday, The Dodge City Bank was very busy. Some people took money out. Others put money in. How much money did each person have in the bank at the end of the day?

1. Wild Bill took out $1.20 to buy a 🤠 .

in the bank $3.30
_____

4. Black Bart took out $1.57 to buy a 🐔 .

in the bank $4.65
_____

2. Jess roped a 🐴 . Earned $5.95.

in the bank $2.10
_____

5. Minnie sold a 🪢 . Earned $6.48

in the bank $4.20
_____

3. Annie took out $3.75 for new 🤠 .

in the bank $5.65
_____

6. Tiny Tom took out $8.25 to buy a 🐴 .

in the bank $9.54
_____

**Make up a word problem of your own. Use these facts:
Cowboy Cal wants to buy a horse.**

88   FS-32021 Math Activities

Skills: Addition, Subtraction, Regrouping

Italian Food Festival

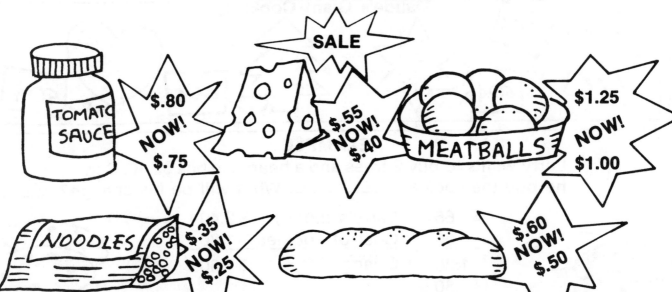

SALE

$.80 NOW! $.75

$.55 NOW! $.40

$1.25 NOW! $1.00

TOMATO SAUCE

MEATBALLS

$.35 NOW! $.25

NOODLES

$.60 NOW! $.50

a. Marilyn bought 2 jars of sauce. How much did she pay? _____ How much did she save? _____

b. Jerry has $3.50. He bought 3 packages of meatballs. How much did they cost? _____ Name something he could buy with his change. _____

c. Tim bought 4 packages of noodles. How much did they cost? _____ Tim gave the checker $2.50. How much change did he get back? _____

d. Sue bought 2 loaves of bread. Ellen bought 3 pieces of cheese. Who spent more money? _____ How much money did Sue save? _____

e. Lynn wants to buy 1 jar of sauce and 2 packages of meatballs. She has $2.50. How much do her groceries cost? _____ How much more money will she need? _____

f. Jim has $2.00. Name 3 different things he could buy with his money.

_____
_____
_____

Maude's Giant Cookies

EXAMPLE

Larry wants to buy 2 trees and a heart. He has $2.40. Can he buy the cookies? _____ What will be his change? _____

$$\begin{array}{l} \$\ .65 \\ +\ .65 \\ \hline 1.30 \\ +\ .50 \\ \hline \$1.80 \end{array}$$

Larry's money $2.40
Cost of cookies – 1.80
Change $ .60

a. Terry has $2.50. He wants to buy 2 gingerbread men and a star. Can he buy them? _____ Tell why or why not. _____

_____

b. Mary gave 3 trees to Sue. She gave 2 stars to Sharon. Which cookies cost more? _____ How much more? _____

c. Jeff has $4.35. Phil has $3.45. Which boy can buy exactly 3 trees and 3 hearts with his money? _____

d. At the end of the day, Maude gives away leftover cookies. Joe paid Maude $1.60. He had 4 stars. How many did he get free? _____

e. Maude put these cookies in packages: 2 stars in one package, 3 trees in another package and 4 hearts in the last package. How much did each package cost? _____, _____, _____. What was the total cost of all the cookies?

_____

f. The gingerbread men are going to be on sale for $.90 each. Jan has $2.75. Can she buy 3 gingerbread men? _____ Can she buy a star too? _____

_____

g. Cory bought 6 hearts. They were all broken so he only paid half price. How much did the cookies cost? _____

Ice Cream Match-Up

8¢   3¢   2¢   4¢   9¢   5¢   7¢

a. _____ b. _____ c. _____ d. _____ e. _____ f. _____ g. _____

Example: Tim bought **4** cones. The total cost was **20¢**. How much did each cone cost? This is how you find out: 4 × _____ = 20¢. Do you know your multiplication tables? If so, the answer will be easy for you to figure out.

Find each child's matching cone. Write his or her name on the line under the correct cone.

Sara bought 2 cones. The total cost was 18¢.

Marie bought 6 cones. The total cost was 24¢.

Dave bought 3 cones. The total cost was 21¢.

Dick bought 5 cones. The total cost was 25¢.

Donna bought 5 cones. The total cost was 10¢.

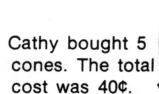  

Cathy bought 5 cones. The total cost was 40¢.

Helen bought 3 cones. The total cost was 9¢.

Bonus: Don has 27¢. He wants to buy 3 ice cream cones. How much will each one cost? _____

FS-32021 Math Activities

Bake Sale

a. We bought 3 muffins. Each one cost 8¢. How much did we spend?

_____ ¢

b. Let's get a cake for the bake sale. We can sell each piece for 5¢. We will cut the cake into 8 pieces. How much will we earn?

_____ ¢

c. Mother bought 5 donuts for breakfast. Each one cost 5¢. How much did Mother spend?

_____ ¢

d. Our class has saved $1.00. We want to buy 10 pumpkin cookies. Each one costs 10¢. Can we buy them? _____
How much will they cost?

_____

e. The tarts are on sale for 10¢ each. I want 4 of them. How much money do I need? _____ ¢

f. How would you like to buy 6 homemade cookies? They only cost 6¢ each. You will need _____ ¢.

g. Lemon pie is my favorite. Each slice costs 10¢. I'm going to buy 3 slices. How much money do I need? _____ ¢

h. That cheese bread looks so good! Each loaf costs 8¢. I have 75¢ and I want to buy 7 loaves. Can I buy them? _____
How much will they cost?

_____ ¢

Bonus: How much change will be left?

_____

Bonus: How much change will I get back?

_____

FS-32021 Math Activities

Write the number sentence and label your answer.

1. John has 20¢. If donuts are 5¢ each, how many can he buy?

$$20 \div 5 = 4$$

John can buy __4__ __donuts__ .

2. The baker made 72 brownies. He put 9 rows of them on a tray. How many were in each row?

_____

Each row had _____ _____ .

3. Sue has 48¢. If cookies are 8¢ each, how many can she buy?

_____

Sue can buy _____ _____ .

4. If Jill buys 24 cream puffs and divides them equally into 4 bags, how many will be in each bag?

_____

Each bag will have _____ .

5. The baker made 12 cake layers. He needs to make three cakes. How many layers will each cake have?

_____

Each will have _____ _____ .

6. Bill has 49¢. If donut holes are 7¢ each, how many can he buy?

_____

Bill can buy _____ _____ .

7. The baker put 56 hot rolls in 8 rows. How many were in each row?

_____

Each row had _____ _____ .

Name _____

Write the number sentence and label your answer.

1. How much more will Bill spend than Sue if:

   a. Bill buys 5 oranges for 8¢ each? _____

   b. Sue buys 4 apples for 9¢ each? _____

   Bill will spend _____ more than Sue.

2. Which is the better buy? (Circle a or b)

   a. Sue's 4 small cans of juice at 7¢ each. _____

   b. Bill's 3 cans of juice at 9¢ each. _____

   How much better? _____

3. What is the cost per pear if:

   a. Bill spends 54¢ for 9 pears. _____

   b. Sue spends 28¢ for 4 pears. _____

   _____ spends _____ more per pear.

4. How much less will be spent per lemon if:

   a. Sue spends 64¢ on 8 lemons. _____

   b. Bill spends 25¢ on 5 lemons. _____

   _____ will spend _____ less per lemon.

5. How much difference in total price is there if:

   a. Bill buys 6 carrots for 7¢ each. _____

   b. Sue buys 5 potatoes for 9¢ each. _____

   There is _____ difference in price.

Look at the time under each clock. Draw the hands in the right place.

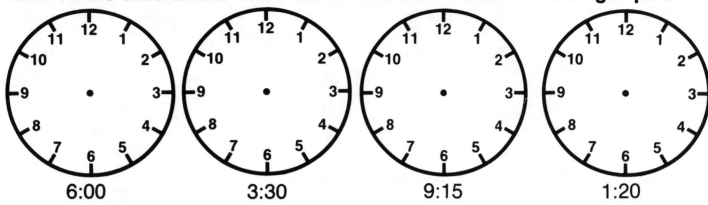

6:00   3:30   9:15   1:20

Write these times using numbers.

1. seven forty-five _____   3. quarter after two _____

2. half past four _____   4. six thirty _____

How many __minutes__ is it after the hour?

_____   _____   _____   _____

Look at the clocks. What time will it be:

two hours later   four hours before   one hour later   seven hours before

_____   _____   _____   _____

95   FS-32021 Math Activities

Name _____

 **1.**  **2.** **3.** **4.** **5.**

Half Dollar
Penny
Quarter
Dime
Nickel

Write the name of each numbered coin.
Tell its value.

1. _____ _____¢   3. _____ _____¢

2. _____ _____¢   4. _____ _____¢

5. _____ _____¢

Change the words into numbers.

6. seventy-five cents _____   10. fifty cents _____

7. thirty cents _____   11. twenty-five cents _____

8. three dollars and
   ten cents _____   12. two dollars and
   thirty-five cents _____

9. five dollars and
   fifteen cents _____   13. one dollar and
   twenty-two cents _____

Write the value of these coins.

14. + + + = _____

15. + + + + = _____

16. + + + + = _____

17. + + + + = _____

96

FS-32021 Math Activities

 = 75¢  = 50¢ = 25¢

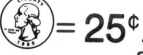

Sam's Snack Shop
Menu

Soup
  Tomato _____¢
  Noodle _____¢

Sandwich
  Tuna _____¢
  Egg _____¢
  Cheese _____¢

Drinks
  Milk _____¢
  Juice _____¢

Find the cost of each food. Write the amount in the ( ) and next to the food on the menu.

	Ate	Paid	
Don	Tomato Soup		( )
Marie	Milk		( )
Jan	Cheese Sandwich		( )
Jerry	Noodle Soup		( )
Rusty	Tuna Sandwich		( )
Laurie	Juice		( )
Lisa	Egg Sandwich		( )

97

FS-32021 Math Activities

Money Madness

Write the correct answer on the line.

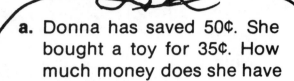

a. Donna has saved 50¢. She bought a toy for 35¢. How much money does she have left? _____

b. This book costs 86¢. Today it is on sale. Now it only costs 75¢. How much money will I save? _____

c. Lynn is going to baby-sit for two nights. She will earn 49¢ on Friday. She will earn 48¢ on Saturday. How much money will she earn all together? _____

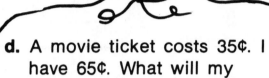

d. A movie ticket costs 35¢. I have 65¢. What will my change be? _____

Solve the problems:

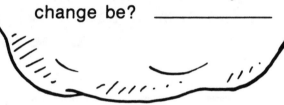

 10¢   20¢   25¢   15¢   30¢

e. Dave has 75¢. He bought an apple and an orange.
Cost: _____ What is his change? _____

f. Leann bought 2 pears and a strawberry.

Cost: _____

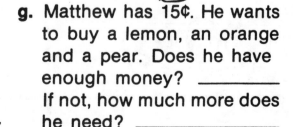

g. Matthew has 15¢. He wants to buy a lemon, an orange and a pear. Does he have enough money? _____
If not, how much more does he need? _____

h. One pear costs 20¢. How much will 3 pears cost? _____ Two apples? _____

98   FS-32021 Math Activities

Name _____

Write the number sentence and label your answer.

16 oz. Steak..... $4.58

Italian Spaghetti... $2.24

Salad...... $1.43

Hamburger $1.32

Milk .31

Coffee .40

May I take your order, please?

1. Dad had steak and a cup of coffee for dinner. How much was his bill? _____ Dad's bill was _____ .	2. Mom had the spaghetti and a salad. How much did she spend? _____ Mom spent _____ .
3. John had $3.68. If he bought a hamburger, how much did he have left? _____ John had _____ left.	4. Sue had a salad and a glass of milk. If she left a 25¢ tip, how much did she spend? _____ Sue spent _____ .
5. How much more did Dad's dinner cost than Mom's? _____ It cost _____ more.	6. How much difference in price is there between the steak dinner and the spaghetti dinner? _____ A difference of _____ .

99   FS-32021 Math Activities

Name _____

Write the number sentence and label your answer.

 Jim's Restaurant

Bacon & Eggs...........$2.65	Muffin...............30
Ham & Eggs.............$3.25	Toast...............35
Steak & Eggs...........$4.80	Cereal 60
Fresh Fruit...............$1.39	Milk 45
Hash Brown Potatoes..... .90	Juice...............75
Pancakes.................$1.75	Coffee.............50

1. Mark had ham and eggs and a glass of milk for breakfast. How much did he spend?

_____

Mark spent _____ .

2. John wants bacon and eggs. How much less will his breakfast cost than Mark's?

_____

It will cost _____ less.

3. Ann had steak and eggs, toast and a glass of juice. How much was her bill?

_____

Ann's bill was _____ .

4. How much more do the ham and eggs cost than the pancakes?

_____

They cost _____ more.

5. Nancy had a muffin with her bacon and eggs. How much was her breakfast?

_____

Her breakfast was _____ .

6. How much difference in price is there between the pancakes and the fresh fruit?

_____

The difference is _____ .

FS-32021 Math Activities

Write the number sentence and label your answer.

1. Mr Adams spent $4.69 for a saw, $2.88 for a hammer, and $1.63 for some nails. How much did he spend in all?

_____

He spent _____ in all.

2. Mr. Jones spent $6.42 on tools. Mr. Robbins spent $4.87 on tools. How much more did Mr. Jones spend than Mr. Robbins?

_____

He spent _____ more.

3. Tom bought 7 packages of hooks. If there were 8 hooks in each package, how many hooks did he buy?

_____

Tom bought ____ _____ .

4. Mrs. Adams looked at a step stool for $3.98 and one for $5.66. How much difference in cost was there?

_____

The difference was _____ .

5. Diane bought 225 large nails and 110 small ones. How many nails did she buy altogether?

_____

Diane bought ____ _____ .

6. Mrs. Robbins bought a package of screws for 48¢. If screws are 6¢ each, how many screws were the package?

_____

There were ____ _____ .

7. The hardware store had 582 gallons of paint in stock. During their sale, 189 gallons were sold. How many are left?

_____

There are ____ _____ left.

FS-32021 Math Activities

Write the number sentence and label your answer.

1. Jim had $2.68 to spend. Linda had $3.45. How much did they have between them?

_____

They had _____ .

2. Jim bought 6 ride tickets. They were 10¢ each. How much was the total cost?

_____

Total cost was _____ .

3. Ann spent $2.60 at a booth. Tom spent $1.75. How much more did Ann spend?

_____

Ann spent _____ more.

4. Linda spent 40¢ on tickets. If they were 5¢ each, how many tickets did she get?

_____

Linda got ____ _____ .

5. Mark spent $5.32 at the park. Mary spent $3.69. How much less did Mary spend than Mark?

_____

Mary spent _____ less.

6. John spent $2.65 on tickets, $1.98 on food, and $3.49 on a toy dog. How much did he spend in all?

_____

John spent _____ in all.

Name _____

Math Path

Follow the directions in each box. Follow the arrow to the next box unless the directions tell you to do something different.

START

Add.

27
+36

Fill in the missing numbers.

5, 10, 15, ___ , 25, 30, ___ , 40, 45, ___ , 55, 60, ___

Color ½ of the next box blue. Color ½ of the box red.

Circle all the odd numbers in this box.

3   4   13   12   7

27   9   8   25   20

What is the largest number you can write using the digits 7, 2, and 9 once?

_____

Write the number in the box that makes the math sentence correct.

12 – ☐ = 4

Subtract.

$ .57
– $ .40

Count the boxes in which you wrote or colored something. Your total should equal 6 + 3.

Write ninety-five as a number.

_____

How many quarters equal one dollar?

_____

In the next box, color the squares green. Color the triangles orange. Color the rectangles purple.

If 82 is larger than 79, skip the next box.

Brainwork! Draw a new box to add to the path. Write a math problem in it.

103

FS-32021 Math Activities

The Math Box Game

Follow the directions in each box. Follow the double lines to the next box unless the directions tell you to do something different.

START

Write three hundred fifty-nine as a number.

_____

In the next box, write the time below each clock.

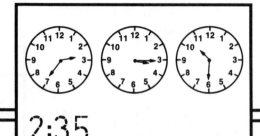

2:35 _____ _____

Subtract.

427
− 185

In the next box, draw a dashed line that shows where you could fold each object so its two sides match exactly.

On each line, draw the next shape in the pattern.

□ o □ o □ __
△ ▽ △ ▽ △ __

Add.

7
6
3
+ 8

Count the boxes in which you wrote or colored something. Your total should equal 18 − 9.

Circle the problems that equal 12.

3 × 5   4 × 3
     17 − 5
8 + 4   12 × 0

Divide the next box into four equal parts, called fourths. Color $\frac{1}{4}$ of the box yellow. Color $\frac{3}{4}$ of the box green.

Shade in five coins that together equal 51¢.

Write this Roman numeral as a number.

VII =

If 5 × 4 equals 20, skip the next box.

Brainwork! Draw a new box for this game. Write a math problem in it.

Answer Key

Each child will need a brad for the clock hands. The clocks can be mounted on tagboard or other stiff paper. Use the clocks with pages 5, 6, 9, 15, 16, 17, 18, and 19 to strengthen and reinforce the concept of telling time.

Page 1

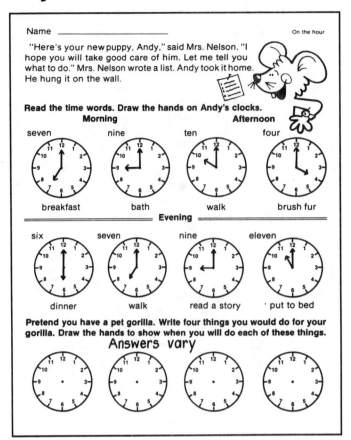

Name _____   On the hour

"Here's your new puppy, Andy," said Mrs. Nelson. "I hope you will take good care of him. Let me tell you what to do." Mrs. Nelson wrote a list. Andy took it home. He hung it on the wall.

Read the time words. Draw the hands on Andy's clocks.

Morning			Afternoon
seven	nine	ten	four
breakfast	bath	walk	brush fur

Evening

| six | seven | nine | eleven |
| dinner | walk | read a story | put to bed |

Pretend you have a pet gorilla. Write four things you would do for your gorilla. Draw the hands to show when you will do each of these things.

Answers vary

Page 2

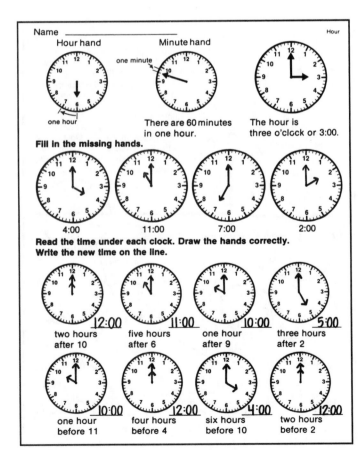

Name _____   Hour

Hour hand   Minute hand

one minute

one hour

There are 60 minutes in one hour.

The hour is three o'clock or 3:00.

Fill in the missing hands.

4:00   11:00   7:00   2:00

Read the time under each clock. Draw the hands correctly. Write the new time on the line.

12:00   11:00   10:00   5:00
two hours after 10 | five hours after 6 | one hour after 9 | three hours after 2

10:00   12:00   4:00   12:00
one hour before 11 | four hours before 4 | six hours before 10 | two hours before 2

Page 3

Name _____ Answers vary   AM and PM

"The show starts at nine o'clock," Ann told her mother. "Is that nine in the morning?"

"Yes, it is," answered Mother. "Do you know how to tell? Look at the letters after nine. It says a.m. That means 'in the morning'. There are twelve morning hours—midnight to twelve noon.

"Another show starts at eight p.m. P.M. means 'in the afternoon or evening'. There are twelve p.m. hours—twelve noon to midnight. Each day has 24 hours."

Morning   Early Morning   Evening   Afternoon

On the line, write the hour that Ann might do each thing. Write a.m. or p.m. Draw the hands on the clock.

| get home from school | eat dinner | play outside | get out of bed |

| go to school | watch TV | eat breakfast | read a story |

Page 4

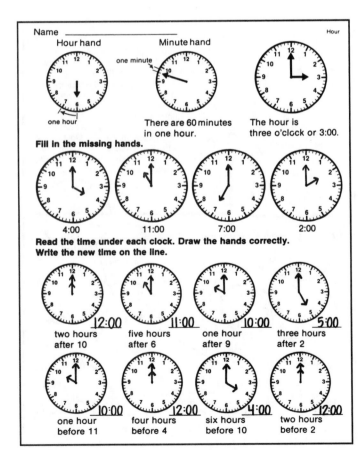

© Frank Schaffer Publications, Inc.   105   FS-32021 Math Activities

Answer Key

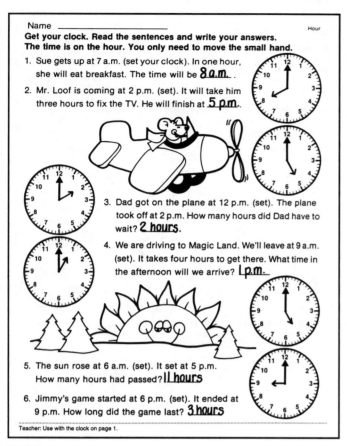

Name _____

Get your clock. Read the sentences and write your answers.
The time is on the hour. You only need to move the small hand.

Hour

1. Sue gets up at 7 a.m. (set your clock). In one hour, she will eat breakfast. The time will be **8 a.m.**

2. Mr. Loof is coming at 2 p.m. (set). It will take him three hours to fix the TV. He will finish at **5 p.m.**

3. Dad got on the plane at 12 p.m. (set). The plane took off at 2 p.m. How many hours did Dad have to wait? **2 hours.**

4. We are driving to Magic Land. We'll leave at 9 a.m. (set). It takes four hours to get there. What time in the afternoon will we arrive? **1 p.m.**

5. The sun rose at 6 a.m. (set). It set at 5 p.m. How many hours had passed? **11 hours**

6. Jimmy's game started at 6 p.m. (set). It ended at 9 p.m. How long did the game last? **3 hours**

Teacher: Use with the clock on page 1.

Page 5

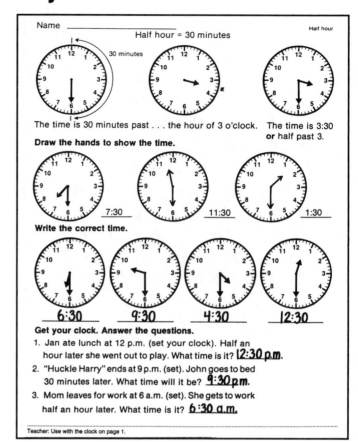

Name _____

Half hour = 30 minutes

Half hour

The time is 30 minutes past . . . the hour of 3 o'clock. The time is 3:30 or half past 3.

Draw the hands to show the time.

7:30   11:30   1:30

Write the correct time.

6:30   9:30   4:30   12:30

Get your clock. Answer the questions.

1. Jan ate lunch at 12 p.m. (set your clock). Half an hour later she went out to play. What time is it? **12:30 p.m.**

2. "Huckle Harry" ends at 9 p.m. (set). John goes to bed 30 minutes later. What time will it be? **9:30 p.m.**

3. Mom leaves for work at 6 a.m. (set). She gets to work half an hour later. What time is it? **6:30 a.m.**

Teacher: Use with the clock on page 1.

Page 6

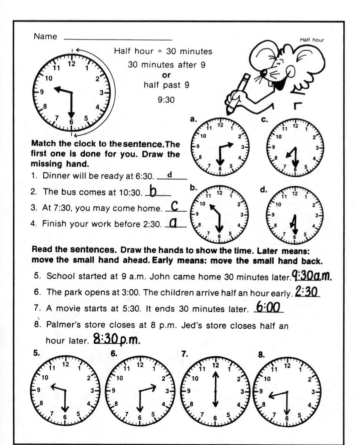

Name _____

Half hour = 30 minutes
30 minutes after 9
or
half past 9
9:30

Half hour

Match the clock to the sentence. The first one is done for you. Draw the missing hand.

1. Dinner will be ready at 6:30. **d**

2. The bus comes at 10:30. **b**

3. At 7:30, you may come home. **c**

4. Finish your work before 2:30. **a**

Read the sentences. Draw the hands to show the time. Later means: move the small hand ahead. Early means: move the small hand back.

5. School started at 9 a.m. John came home 30 minutes later. **9:30 a.m.**

6. The park opens at 3:00. The children arrive half an hour early. **2:30**

7. A movie starts at 5:30. It ends 30 minutes later. **6:00**

8. Palmer's store closes at 8 p.m. Jed's store closes half an hour later. **8:30 p.m.**

5.   6.   7.   8.

Page 7

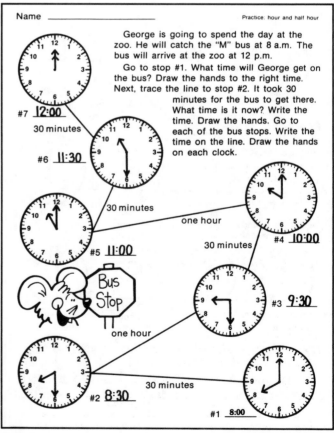

Name _____

Practice: hour and half hour

George is going to spend the day at the zoo. He will catch the "M" bus at 8 a.m. The bus will arrive at the zoo at 12 p.m.

Go to stop #1. What time will George get on the bus? Draw the hands to the right time. Next, trace the line to stop #2. It took 30 minutes for the bus to get there. What time is it now? Write the time. Draw the hands. Go to each of the bus stops. Write the time on the line. Draw the hands on each clock.

#7 **12:00**
30 minutes
#6 **11:30**
30 minutes
#5 **11:00**
one hour
#4 **10:00**
30 minutes
#3 **9:30**
one hour
#2 **8:30**
30 minutes
#1 **8:00**

Bus Stop

Page 8

Answer Key

Fifteen after the hour

1. **2.** **3.**

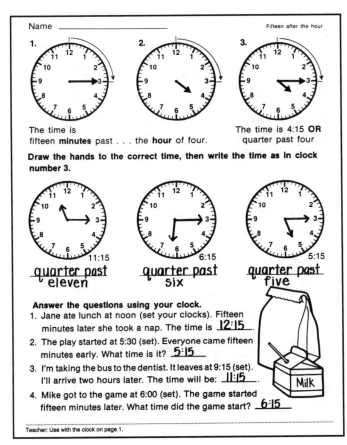

The time is
fifteen **minutes** past . . . the **hour** of four.

The time is 4:15 **OR**
quarter past four

**Draw the hands to the correct time, then write the time as in clock
number 3.**

11:15   6:15   5:15

**quarter past
eleven**   **quarter past
six**   **quarter past
five**

Answer the questions using your clock.

1. Jane ate lunch at noon (set your clocks). Fifteen
   minutes later she took a nap. The time is **12:15**

2. The play started at 5:30 (set). Everyone came fifteen
   minutes early. What time is it? **5:15**

3. I'm taking the bus to the dentist. It leaves at 9:15 (set).
   I'll arrive two hours later. The time will be: **11:15**

4. Mike got to the game at 6:00 (set). The game started
   fifteen minutes later. What time did the game start? **6:15**

Teacher: Use with the clock on page 1.

Page 9

Fifteen before the hour
(mins. = minutes)

→ 15 minutes

The time is fifteen
minutes **before** . . . the hour of seven   **OR** quarter to seven

45 minutes

The time is 45 minutes **after** . . . the hour of six **OR** 6:45

Look at the time under each clock. Draw the hands in the right place.

quarter to one   45 minutes
after four   10:45   quarter to six

2:45   8:45   45 mins. after two   quarter to five

Page 10

Mixed Practice:
Half hour; quarter hour

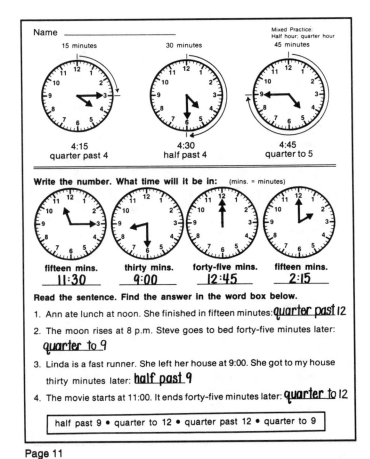

15 minutes   30 minutes   45 minutes

4:15
quarter past 4   4:30
half past 4   4:45
quarter to 5

Write the number. What time will it be in: (mins. = minutes)

fifteen mins.
11:30   **thirty mins.**
9:00   **forty-five mins.**
12:45   **fifteen mins.**
2:15

Read the sentence. Find the answer in the word box below.

1. Ann ate lunch at noon. She finished in fifteen minutes: **quarter past 12**

2. The moon rises at 8 p.m. Steve goes to bed forty-five minutes later:
   quarter to 9

3. Linda is a fast runner. She left her house at 9:00. She got to my house
   thirty minutes later: **half past 9**

4. The movie starts at 11:00. It ends forty-five minutes later: **quarter to 12**

| half past 9 • quarter to 12 • quarter past 12 • quarter to 9 |

Page 11

Mixed Practice:
half hour; quarter hours

**Write the time shown on the clock: (1) quarter to; quarter past; half past.
(2) Write the time using numbers. For example: quarter to ten - 9:45**

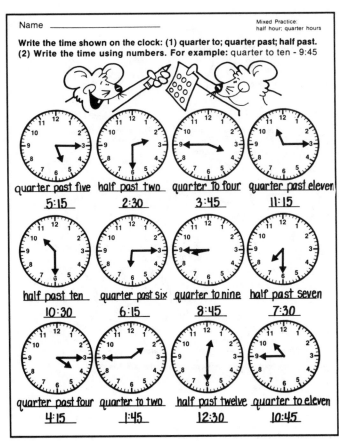

quarter past five   half past two   quarter to four   quarter past eleven
5:15   **2:30**   **3:45**   **11:15**

half past ten   quarter past six   quarter to nine   half past seven
10:30   **6:15**   **8:45**   **7:30**

quarter past four   quarter to two   half past twelve   quarter to eleven
4:15   **1:45**   **12:30**   **10:45**

Page 12

Answer Key

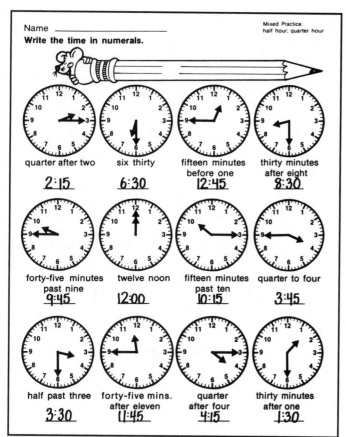

Name _____

Write the time in numerals.

quarter after two	six thirty	fifteen minutes before one	thirty minutes after eight
2:15	6:30	12:45	8:30

forty-five minutes past nine	twelve noon	fifteen minutes past ten	quarter to four
9:45	12:00	10:15	3:45

half past three	forty-five mins. after eleven	quarter after four	thirty minutes after one
3:30	11:45	4:15	1:30

Page 13

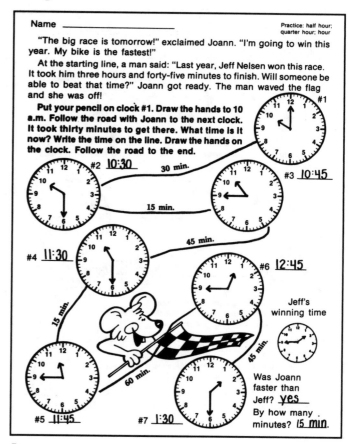

Name _____

"The big race is tomorrow!" exclaimed Joann. "I'm going to win this year. My bike is the fastest!"

At the starting line, a man said: "Last year, Jeff Nelsen won this race. It took him three hours and forty-five minutes to finish. Will someone be able to beat that time?" Joann got ready. The man waved the flag and she was off!

Put your pencil on clock #1. Draw the hands to 10 a.m. Follow the road with Joann to the next clock. It took thirty minutes to get there. What time is it now? Write the time on the line. Draw the hands on the clock. Follow the road to the end.

#1
#2 10:30   30 min.   #3 10:45
15 min.
45 min.
#4 11:30   #6 12:45
15 min.
Jeff's winning time
45 min.
#5 11:45   60 min.   Was Joann faster than Jeff? **yes**
#7 1:30   By how many minutes? **15 min.**

Page 14

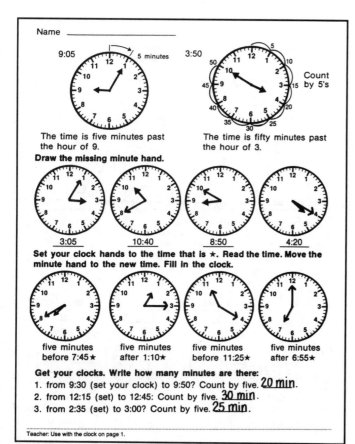

Name _____

9:05 — 5 minutes

The time is five minutes past the hour of 9.

3:50   Count by 5's

The time is fifty minutes past the hour of 3.

Draw the missing minute hand.

3:05	10:40	8:50	4:20

Set your clock hands to the time that is ★. Read the time. Move the minute hand to the new time. Fill in the clock.

five minutes before 7:45★	five minutes after 1:10★	five minutes before 11:25★	five minutes after 6:55★

Get your clocks. Write how many minutes are there:
1. from 9:30 (set your clock) to 9:50? Count by five. **20 min.**
2. from 12:15 (set) to 12:45: Count by five. **30 min.**
3. from 2:35 (set) to 3:00? Count by five. **25 min.**

Page 15

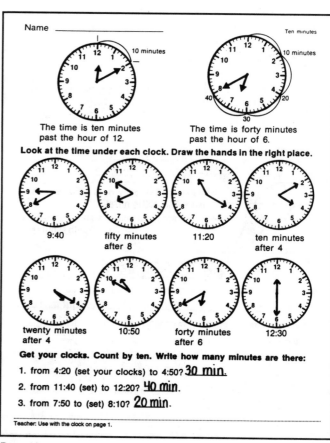

Name _____

10 minutes

The time is ten minutes past the hour of 12.

10 minutes

The time is forty minutes past the hour of 6.

Look at the time under each clock. Draw the hands in the right place.

9:40	fifty minutes after 8	11:20	ten minutes after 4

twenty minutes after 4	10:50	forty minutes after 6	12:30

Get your clocks. Count by ten. Write how many minutes are there:
1. from 4:20 (set your clocks) to 4:50? **30 min.**
2. from 11:40 (set) to 12:20? **40 min.**
3. from 7:50 to (set) 8:10? **20 min.**

Page 16

Answer Key

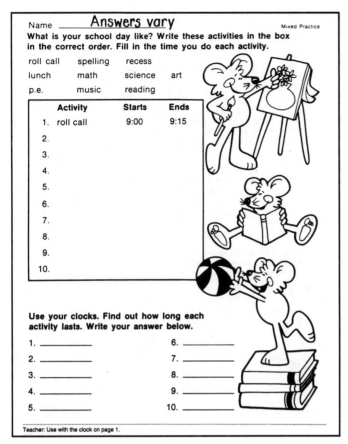

Name _____

Answers vary

Mixed Practice

What is your school day like? Write these activities in the box in the correct order. Fill in the time you do each activity.

roll call	spelling	recess
lunch	math	science	art
p.e.	music	reading

	Activity	Starts	Ends
1.	roll call	9:00	9:15
2.			
3.			
4.			
5.			
6.			
7.			
8.			
9.			
10.			

Use your clocks. Find out how long each activity lasts. Write your answer below.

1. _____   6. _____
2. _____   7. _____
3. _____   8. _____
4. _____   9. _____
5. _____   10. _____

Teacher: Use with the clock on page 1.

Page 17

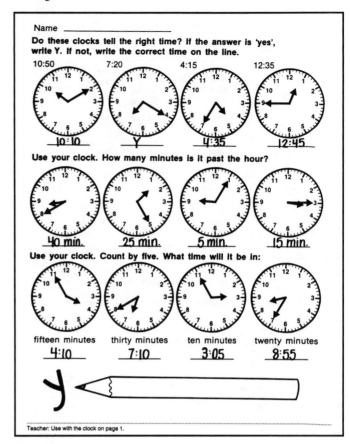

Name _____

Do these clocks tell the right time? If the answer is 'yes', write Y. If not, write the correct time on the line.

10:50 — **10:10**   7:20 — **Y**   4:15 — **4:35**   12:35 — **12:45**

Use your clock. How many minutes is it past the hour?

40 min.   **25 min.**   **5 min.**   **15 min.**

Use your clock. Count by five. What time will it be in:

fifteen minutes **4:10**   thirty minutes **7:10**   ten minutes **3:05**   twenty minutes **8:55**

Teacher: Use with the clock on page 1.

Page 18

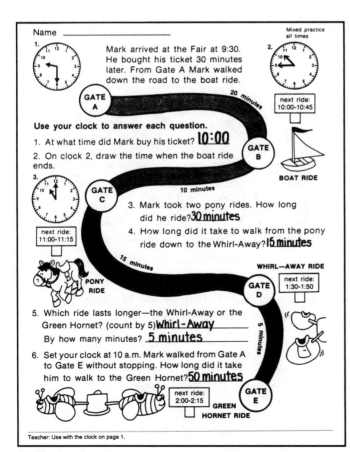

Name _____

Mixed practice all times

Mark arrived at the Fair at 9:30. He bought his ticket 30 minutes later. From Gate A Mark walked down the road to the boat ride.

GATE A

20 minutes

next ride: 10:00-10:45

GATE B

BOAT RIDE

Use your clock to answer each question.

1. At what time did Mark buy his ticket? **10:00**

2. On clock 2, draw the time when the boat ride ends.

GATE C

10 minutes

next ride: 11:00-11:15

3. Mark took two pony rides. How long did he ride? **30 minutes**

4. How long did it take to walk from the pony ride down to the Whirl-Away? **15 minutes**

15 minutes

PONY RIDE

WHIRL—AWAY RIDE

GATE D

next ride: 1:30-1:50

5. Which ride lasts longer—the Whirl-Away or the Green Hornet? (count by 5) **Whirl-Away**
   By how many minutes? **5 minutes**

5 minutes

6. Set your clock at 10 a.m. Mark walked from Gate A to Gate E without stopping. How long did it take him to walk to the Green Hornet? **50 minutes**

next ride: 2:00-2:15

GATE E

GREEN HORNET RIDE

Teacher: Use with the clock on page 1.

Page 19

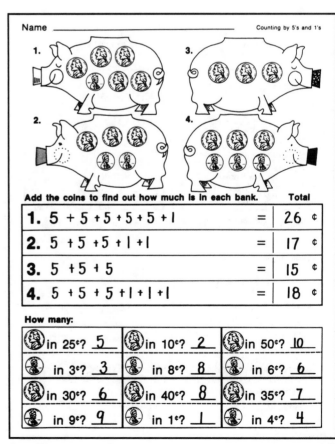

Name _____

Counting by 5's and 1's

1.   3.

2.   4.

Add the coins to find out how much is in each bank.   Total

		Total
1. 5 + 5 + 5 + 5 + 1	=	26 ¢
2. 5 + 5 + 5 + 1 + 1	=	17 ¢
3. 5 + 5 + 5	=	15 ¢
4. 5 + 5 + 5 + 1 + 1 + 1	=	18 ¢

How many:

in 25¢? **5**	in 10¢? **2**	in 50¢? **10**
in 3¢? **3**	in 8¢? **8**	in 6¢? **6**
in 30¢? **6**	in 40¢? **8**	in 35¢? **7**
in 9¢? **9**	in 1¢? **1**	in 4¢? **4**

Page 20

Answer Key

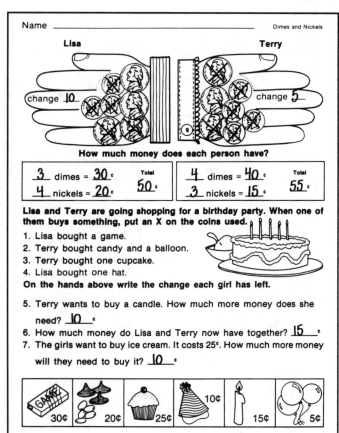

Page 21

Name _____ Dimes and Nickels

Lisa — Terry

change 10   change 5

How much money does each person have?

3 dimes = 30¢
4 nickels = 20¢
Total 50¢

4 dimes = 40¢
3 nickels = 15¢
Total 55¢

Lisa and Terry are going shopping for a birthday party. When one of them buys something, put an X on the coins used.

1. Lisa bought a game.
2. Terry bought candy and a balloon.
3. Terry bought one cupcake.
4. Lisa bought one hat.

On the hands above write the change each girl has left.

5. Terry wants to buy a candle. How much more money does she need? 10 ¢
6. How much money do Lisa and Terry now have together? 15 ¢
7. The girls want to buy ice cream. It costs 25¢. How much more money will they need to buy it? 10 ¢

GAME 30¢   20¢   25¢   10¢   15¢   5¢

Page 22

Name _____ Dimes, Nickels, Pennies

Add the coins. Find out how much each item costs.

Price 27¢   Price 35¢

Price 58¢   Price 60¢

Find the number of dimes and nickels there are in the starred (*) numbers. Add the cost. Write the price on the tag.

Dimes	Nickels	Price
9	1	* 90¢ +*5¢ = 95

Dimes	Nickels	Price
7	4	* 70¢ +*20¢ = 90

Dimes	Nickels	Price
6	2	* 60¢ +*10¢ = 70

Dimes	Nickels	Price
5	3	* 50¢ +*15¢ = 65

SALE

Dimes	Nickels	Price
3	6	* 30¢ +*30¢ = 60

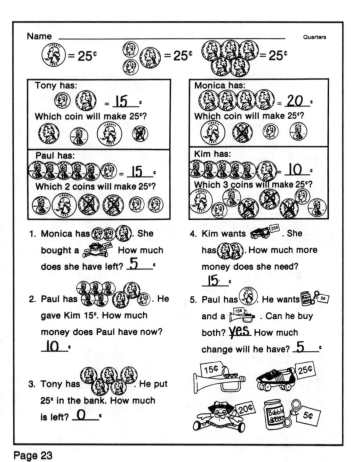

Page 23

Name _____ Quarters

= 25¢   = 25¢   = 25¢

Tony has: = 15¢
Which coin will make 25¢?

Monica has: = 20¢
Which coin will make 25¢?

Paul has: = 15¢
Which 2 coins will make 25¢?

Kim has: = 10¢
Which 3 coins will make 25¢?

1. Monica has ⊙⊙. She bought a ▭. How much does she have left? 5 ¢

2. Paul has ⊙⊙⊙. He gave Kim 15¢. How much money does Paul have now? 10 ¢

3. Tony has ⊙⊙⊙. He put 25¢ in the bank. How much is left? 0 ¢

4. Kim wants 25¢. She has ⊙⊙. How much more money does she need? 15 ¢

5. Paul has ⊙. He wants ▭ 5¢ and a ▭ 15¢. Can he buy both? yes How much change will he have? 5 ¢

15¢   25¢   20¢   5¢

Page 24

Name _____ More And Less

35¢

20¢   25¢   30¢   40¢
1¢   15¢   10¢
5¢

Can you buy: yes/no   more/less

1. A 🍪 with a 🪙 ? no It costs more than a 🪙.
2. A 🧁 with a 🪙 ? no It costs more than a 🪙.
3. A ◯ with a 🪙 ? yes It costs less than a 🪙.
4. A ▱ with a 🪙 ? no It costs more than a 🪙.

Do you need more or less money?

5. You have 🪙🪙 to buy a ☺. less
6. You have 🪙🪙🪙 to buy a 🧁. more
7. You have 🪙 to buy a 🍞. more
8. You have 🪙🪙 to buy a 🍪. more
9. You have 🪙 to buy a ⭐. less
10. You have 🪙🪙 to buy a 🥧. more

FS-32021 Math Activities

Answer Key

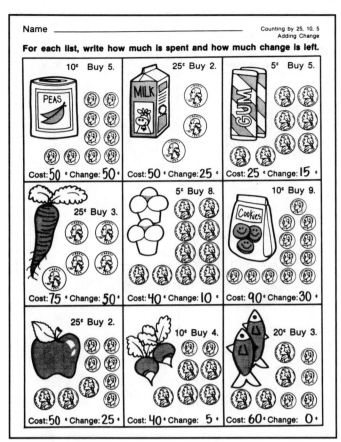

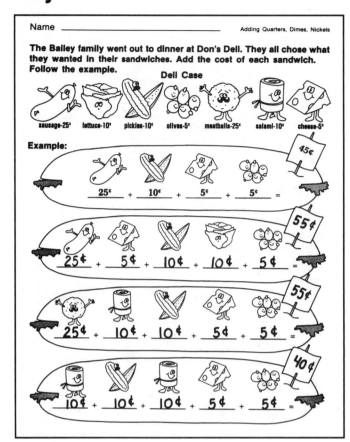

Page 25

Page 26

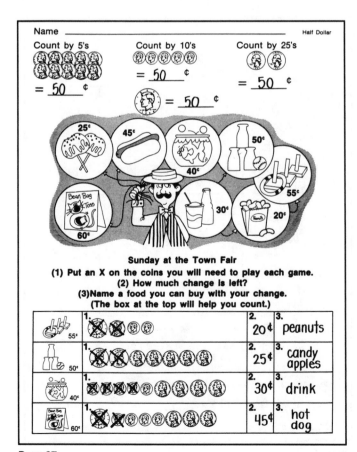

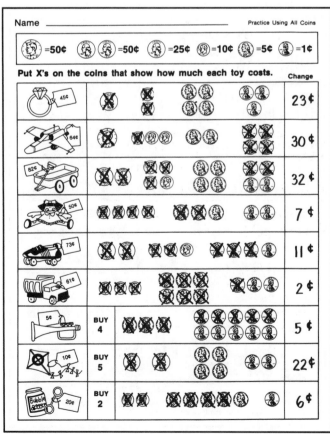

Page 27

Page 28

Answer Key

Page 29

Name _____ Parts of a Dollar

Count by 10	Count by 25	Count by 50	
10 dimes = $1.00	4 quarters = $1.00	2 half dollars = $1.00	$1.00

Each grocery order must total $1.00. (1) What coins will you need? Write Q, D, or HD on the line. (2) Write the value of each coin in the box.

Q
75¢ + 25¢ = $1.00

HD
50¢ + 50¢ = $1.00

HD
50¢ + 50¢ = $1.00

HD
50¢ + 50¢ = $1.00

Q
75¢ + 25¢ = $1.00

HD
50¢ + 50¢ = $1.00

Page 29

Page 30

Name _____ Parts of a Dollar

20 = $1.00   10 = $1.00   4 = $1.00   2 = $1.00

Write the cost of each toy. Color the toys that cost exactly $1.00.

1 = 50¢
2 = 50¢
Total: $1.00

2 = 50¢
4 = 40¢
Total: 90¢

10 = 50¢
5 = 50¢
Total: $1.00

3 = 75¢
1 = 10¢
Total: 85¢

2 = 50¢
5 = 50¢
Total: $1.00

1 = 50¢
5 = 50¢
Total: $1.00

Page 30

Page 31

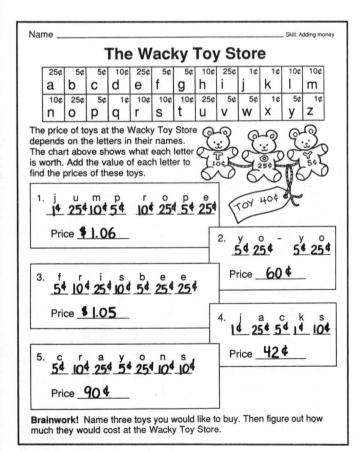

Name _____ Skill: Adding money

The Wacky Toy Store

25¢	5¢	5¢	10¢	25¢	5¢	5¢	10¢	25¢	1¢	1¢	10¢	10¢
a	b	c	d	e	f	g	h	i	j	k	l	m

10¢	25¢	5¢	1¢	10¢	10¢	10¢	25¢	5¢	5¢	1¢	5¢	1¢
n	o	p	q	r	s	t	u	v	w	x	y	z

The price of toys at the Wacky Toy Store depends on the letters in their names. The chart above shows what each letter is worth. Add the value of each letter to find the prices of these toys.

TOY 40¢

1. j u m p r o p e
   1¢ 25¢ 10¢ 5¢ 10¢ 25¢ 5¢ 25¢
   Price $1.06

2. y o - y o
   5¢ 25¢ 5¢ 25¢
   Price 60¢

3. f r i s b e e
   5¢ 10¢ 25¢ 10¢ 5¢ 25¢ 25¢
   Price $1.05

4. j a c k s
   1¢ 25¢ 5¢ 1¢ 10¢
   Price 42¢

5. c r a y o n s
   5¢ 10¢ 25¢ 5¢ 25¢ 10¢ 10¢
   Price 90¢

Brainwork! Name three toys you would like to buy. Then figure out how much they would cost at the Wacky Toy Store.

Page 31

Page 32

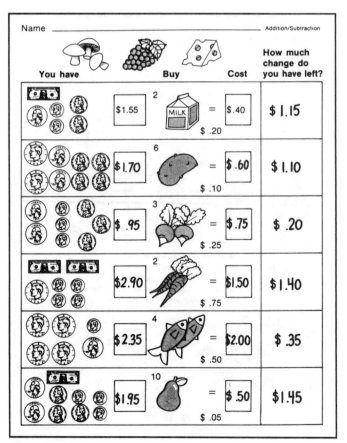

Name _____ Addition/Subtraction

You have	Buy	Cost	How much change do you have left?
$1.55	2 MILK $.20	$.40	$1.15
$1.70	6 $.10	$.60	$1.10
$.95	3 $.25	$.75	$.20
$2.90	2 $.75	$1.50	$1.40
$2.35	4 $.50	$2.00	$.35
$1.95	10 $.05	$.50	$1.45

Page 32

112

FS-32021 Math Activities

Answer Key

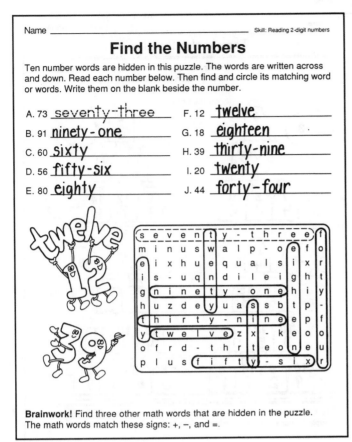

Find the Numbers

Ten number words are hidden in this puzzle. The words are written across and down. Read each number below. Then find and circle its matching word or words. Write them on the blank beside the number.

A. 73 seventy-three

B. 91 ninety-one

C. 60 sixty

D. 56 fifty-six

E. 80 eighty

F. 12 twelve

G. 18 eighteen

H. 39 thirty-nine

I. 20 twenty

J. 44 forty-four

Brainwork! Find three other math words that are hidden in the puzzle. The math words match these signs: +, –, and =.

Page 33

Math Maze

Count by twos to make your way through this maze to the circled number. You can move up, down, across, or diagonally one box at a time. Draw a line that shows your path.

This time count by fives. Remember to mark your path!

Brainwork! Count backwards by fives from 100 to 5. Write the numbers as you count.

Page 34

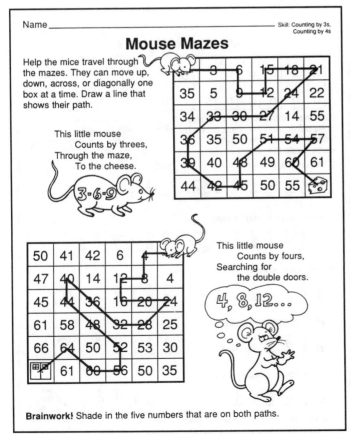

Mouse Mazes

Help the mice travel through the mazes. They can move up, down, across, or diagonally one box at a time. Draw a line that shows their path.

This little mouse
Counts by threes,
Through the maze,
To the cheese.

This little mouse
Counts by fours,
Searching for
the double doors.

4, 8, 12...

Brainwork! Shade in the five numbers that are on both paths.

Page 35

On Target

Be on target with your addition facts. In each box write the missing sum.

Try This! Create word problems for three of the addition facts above. Ask a friend to solve them.

Page 36

Answer Key

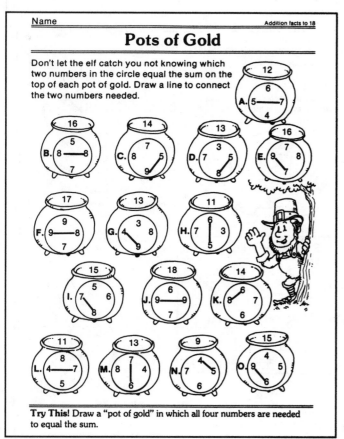

Pots of Gold

Don't let the elf catch you not knowing which two numbers in the circle equal the sum on the top of each pot of gold. Draw a line to connect the two numbers needed.

Try This! Draw a "pot of gold" in which all four numbers are needed to equal the sum.

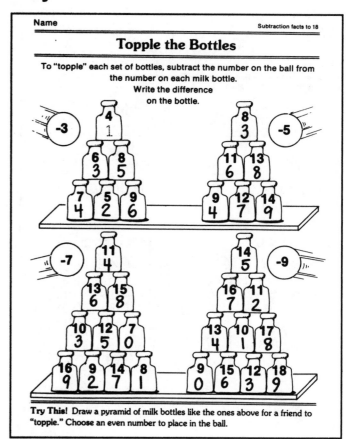

Topple the Bottles

To "topple" each set of bottles, subtract the number on the ball from the number on each milk bottle.
Write the difference on the bottle.

Try This! Draw a pyramid of milk bottles like the ones above for a friend to "topple." Choose an even number to place in the ball.

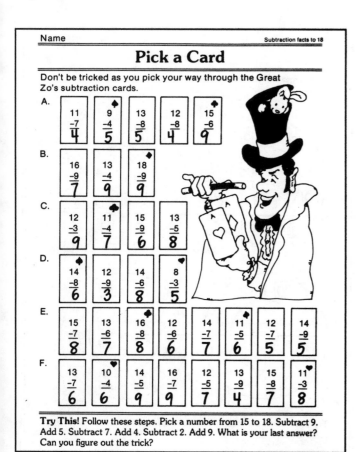

Pick a Card

Don't be tricked as you pick your way through the Great Zo's subtraction cards.

A.
11	9	13	12	15
−7	−4	−8	−8	−6
4	5	5	4	9

B.
16	13	18
−9	−4	−9
7	9	9

C.
12	11	15	13
−3	−4	−9	−5
9	7	6	8

D.
14	12	14	8
−8	−9	−6	−3
6	3	8	5

E.
15	13	16	12	14	11	12	14
−7	−6	−8	−6	−7	−5	−7	−9
8	7	8	6	7	6	5	5

F.
13	10	14	16	12	13	15	11
−7	−4	−5	−7	−5	−9	−8	−3
6	6	9	9	7	4	7	8

Try This! Follow these steps. Pick a number from 15 to 18. Subtract 9. Add 5. Subtract 7. Add 4. Subtract 2. Add 9. What is your last answer? Can you figure out the trick?

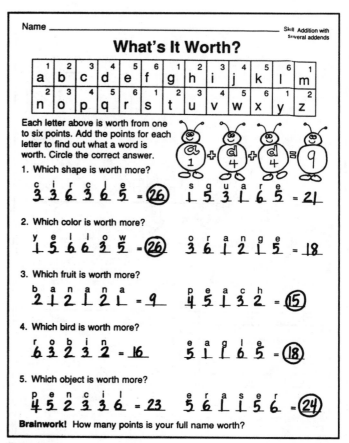

What's It Worth?

1	2	3	4	5	6	1	2	3	4	5	6	1
a	b	c	d	e	f	g	h	i	j	k	l	m

2	3	4	5	6	1	2	3	4	5	6	1	2
n	o	p	q	r	s	t	u	v	w	x	y	z

Each letter above is worth from one to six points. Add the points for each letter to find out what a word is worth. Circle the correct answer.

1. Which shape is worth more?
   c i r c l e
   3 3 6 3 6 5 = (26)   s q u a r e
   1 5 3 1 6 5 = 21

2. Which color is worth more?
   y e l l o w
   1 5 6 6 3 5 = (26)   o r a n g e
   3 6 1 2 1 5 = 18

3. Which fruit is worth more?
   b a n a n a
   2 1 2 1 2 1 = 9   p e a c h
   4 5 1 3 2 = (15)

4. Which bird is worth more?
   r o b i n
   6 3 2 3 2 = 16   e a g l e
   5 1 1 6 5 = (18)

5. Which object is worth more?
   p e n c i l
   4 5 2 3 3 6 = 23   e r a s e r
   5 6 1 5 6 = (24)

Brainwork! How many points is your full name worth?

Answer Key

Stack o' Blocks

Add the numbers on each stack of blocks. Use the key to write a letter below each answer to find a message.

Key	
A=18	I=20	O=10	T=6
B=17	K=13	P=9	U=5
C=16	L=12	R=8	Y=4
E=15	M=11	S=7	
G=21	N=19	H=14	

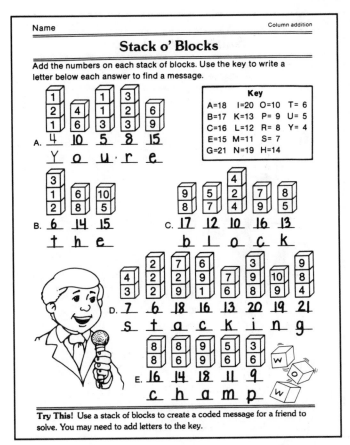

A. 4 10 5 8 15
   Y o u r e

B. 6 14 15
   t h e

C. 17 12 10 16 13
   b l o c k

D. 7 6 18 16 13 20 19 21
   s t a c k i n g

E. 16 14 18 11 9
   c h a m p

Try This! Use a stack of blocks to create a coded message for a friend to solve. You may need to add letters to the key.

Page 41

Subtraction Maze

Work each problem. To find a path to the end of the pie-eating contest, begin at START. Color all the boxes whose answers are even numbers.

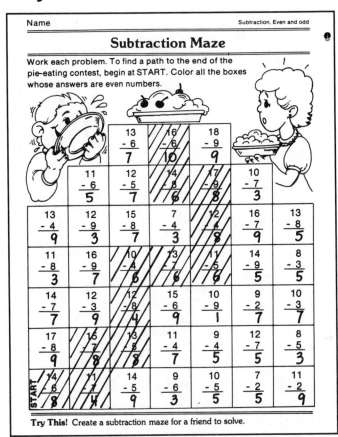

Try This! Create a subtraction maze for a friend to solve.

Page 42

Siz-z-zler Addition

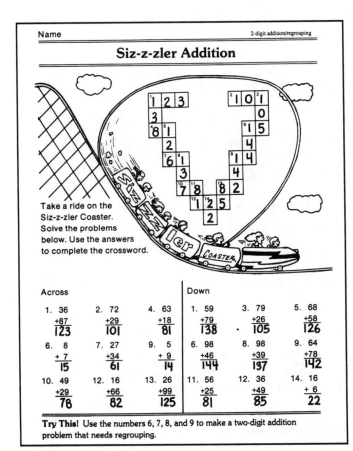

Take a ride on the Siz-z-zler Coaster. Solve the problems below. Use the answers to complete the crossword.

Across

1. 36 +87 = 123
2. 72 +29 = 101
4. 63 +18 = 81
6. 8 + 7 = 15
7. 27 +34 = 61
9. 5 + 9 = 14
10. 49 +29 = 78
12. 16 +66 = 82
13. 26 +99 = 125

Down

1. 59 +79 = 138
3. 79 +26 = 105
5. 68 +58 = 126
6. 98 +46 = 144
8. 98 +39 = 137
9. 64 +78 = 142
11. 56 +25 = 81
12. 36 +49 = 85
14. 16 + 6 = 22

Try This! Use the numbers 6, 7, 8, and 9 to make a two-digit addition problem that needs regrouping.

Page 43

Addin' With Dragon

Mr. Dragon will be braggin' when you fill in each box with the number that correctly completes the problem.

Try This! Complete the pattern: 2, 14, 26, ____, ____, ____ . Now create a different pattern for a friend to try.

Page 44

Answer Key

Page 45

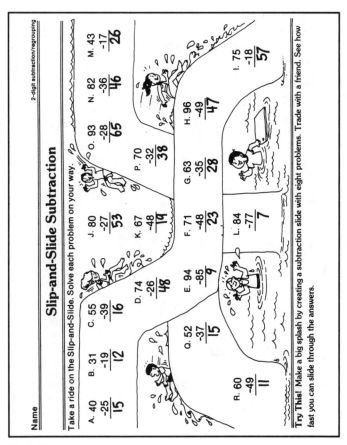

2-digit subtraction/regrouping

Slip-and-Slide Subtraction

Take a ride on the Slip-and-Slide. Solve each problem on your way.

A. 40
-25
15

B. 31
-19
12

C. 55
-39
16

D. 74
-26
48

E. 94
-85
9

F. 71
-48
23

G. 63
-35
28

H. 96
-49
47

I. 75
-18
57

J. 80
-27
53

K. 67
-48
19

L. 84
-77
7

M. 43
-17
26

N. 82
-36
46

O. 93
-28
65

P. 70
-32
38

Q. 52
-37
15

R. 60
-49
11

Try This! Make a big splash by creating a subtraction slide with eight problems. Trade with a friend. See how fast you can slide through the answers.

Page 46

2-digit subtraction, regrouping

Subtraction Action

Protect Subtraction Woman from the five evil crystals. You'll recognize them — they're the ones with the subtraction mistakes. Correct the answers and color the five evil crystals yellow.

90
-26
64

51
-33
18

30
-15
15

73
-27
46

57
-39
18

70
-27
43

92
-84
8

68
-49
19

36
-17
19

54
-27
27

55
-18
37

80
-32
48

41
-24
17

70
-53
17

87
-39
48

44
-18
26

Try This! Using these four digits (8, 2, 3, 5), create and solve two 2-digit subtraction problems that require regrouping.

Page 47

Skill: Addition facts, Subtraction facts

Secret Code

Fill in each box with the number that solves the math sentence.

Add.

7 + 8 = [A]15

5 + 6 = [D]11

8 + [E]5 = 13

9 + [K]9 = 18

[M]0 + 10 = 10

[N]4 + 8 = 12

Subtract.

14 − 8 = [O]6

17 − 9 = [R]8

10 − [S]3 = 7

11 − [T]7 = 4

[U]12 − 6 = 6

[Y]13 − 4 = 9

Write the answer to the riddle.
Use the letters in the code boxes to help you.

What kinds of keys won't fit in your pocket?

d o n k e y s ,
11 6 4 9 5 13 3

m o n k e y s ,
0 6 4 9 5 13 3

a n d t u r k e y s
15 4 11 7 12 8 9 5 13 3

Page 48

Skill: Addition, Subtraction, Following directions

Look Closely

Use the picture to work each problem below. Write the numbers on the lines. Write the addition or subtraction signs in the circles. Mark the final answer in the box.

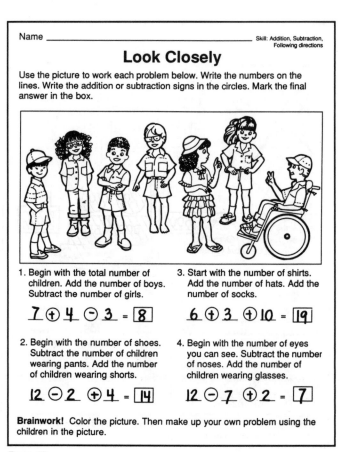

1. Begin with the total number of children. Add the number of boys. Subtract the number of girls.

7 (+) 4 (−) 3 = [8]

2. Begin with the number of shoes. Subtract the number of children wearing pants. Add the number of children wearing shorts.

12 (−) 2 (+) 4 = [14]

3. Start with the number of shirts. Add the number of hats. Add the number of socks.

6 (+) 3 (+) 10 = [19]

4. Begin with the number of eyes you can see. Subtract the number of noses. Add the number of children wearing glasses.

12 (−) 7 (+) 2 = [7]

Brainwork! Color the picture. Then make up your own problem using the children in the picture.

Answer Key

Hocus, Pocus!

Name _____ 2 digit addition/subtraction, regrouping

The wizard has created some gifts for you! First add, then subtract the two numbers in the stars on each gift. (Hint: Remember to place the larger number on top when you subtract.)

A: 38, 57 → 57 + 38 = 95, 57 − 38 = 19
B: 27, 63 → 63 + 27 = 90, 63 − 27 = 36
C: 66, 19 → 66 + 19 = 85, 66 − 19 = 47
D: 17, 46 → 46 + 17 = 63, 46 − 17 = 29
E: 58, 29 → 58 + 29 = 87, 58 − 29 = 29
F: 75, 16 → 75 + 16 = 91, 75 − 16 = 59
G: 37, 53 → 53 + 37 = 90, 53 − 37 = 16
H: 18, 64 → 64 + 18 = 82, 64 − 18 = 46
I: 76, 17 → 76 + 17 = 93, 76 − 17 = 59
J: 39, 55 → 55 + 39 = 94, 55 − 39 = 16

Try This! Pretend that you are the wizard and prepare a little "gift" for a classmate. Using the numbers 5, 6, 7, and 8, create two addition and two subtraction problems for a friend to solve.

Page 49

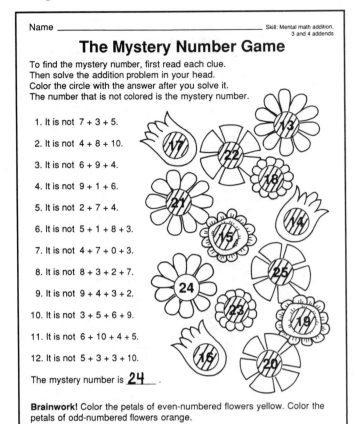

The Mystery Number Game

Name _____ Skill: Mental math addition, 3 and 4 addends

To find the mystery number, first read each clue. Then solve the addition problem in your head. Color the circle with the answer after you solve it. The number that is not colored is the mystery number.

1. It is not 7 + 3 + 5.
2. It is not 4 + 8 + 10.
3. It is not 6 + 9 + 4.
4. It is not 9 + 1 + 6.
5. It is not 2 + 7 + 4.
6. It is not 5 + 1 + 8 + 3.
7. It is not 4 + 7 + 0 + 3.
8. It is not 8 + 3 + 2 + 7.
9. It is not 9 + 4 + 3 + 2.
10. It is not 3 + 5 + 6 + 9.
11. It is not 6 + 10 + 4 + 5.
12. It is not 5 + 3 + 3 + 10.

The mystery number is **24**.

Brainwork! Color the petals of even-numbered flowers yellow. Color the petals of odd-numbered flowers orange.

Page 50

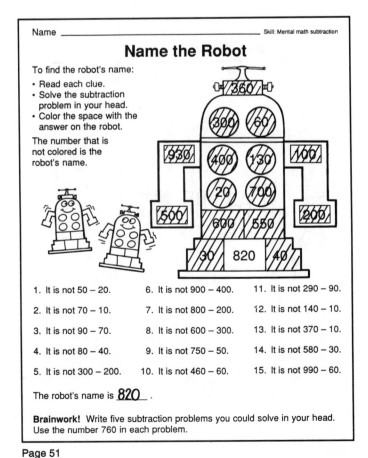

Name the Robot

Name _____ Skill: Mental math subtraction

To find the robot's name:
• Read each clue.
• Solve the subtraction problem in your head.
• Color the space with the answer on the robot.

The number that is not colored is the robot's name.

1. It is not 50 − 20.
2. It is not 70 − 10.
3. It is not 90 − 70.
4. It is not 80 − 40.
5. It is not 300 − 200.
6. It is not 900 − 400.
7. It is not 800 − 200.
8. It is not 600 − 300.
9. It is not 750 − 50.
10. It is not 460 − 60.
11. It is not 290 − 90.
12. It is not 140 − 10.
13. It is not 370 − 10.
14. It is not 580 − 30.
15. It is not 990 − 60.

The robot's name is **820**.

Brainwork! Write five subtraction problems you could solve in your head. Use the number 760 in each problem.

Page 51

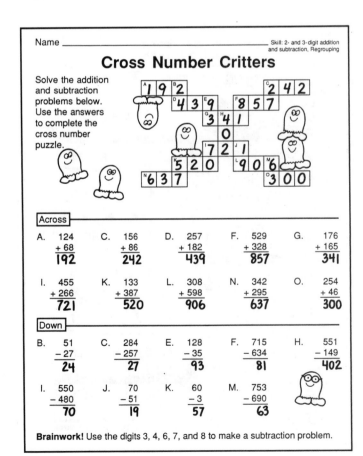

Cross Number Critters

Name _____ Skill: 2- and 3-digit addition and subtraction, Regrouping

Solve the addition and subtraction problems below. Use the answers to complete the cross number puzzle.

Across

A. 124 + 68 = 192
C. 156 + 86 = 242
D. 257 + 182 = 439
F. 529 + 328 = 857
G. 176 + 165 = 341
I. 455 + 266 = 721
K. 133 + 387 = 520
L. 308 + 598 = 906
N. 342 + 295 = 637
O. 254 + 46 = 300

Down

B. 51 − 27 = 24
C. 284 − 257 = 27
E. 128 − 35 = 93
F. 715 − 634 = 81
H. 551 − 149 = 402
I. 550 − 480 = 70
J. 70 − 51 = 19
K. 60 − 3 = 57
M. 753 − 690 = 63

Brainwork! Use the digits 3, 4, 6, 7, and 8 to make a subtraction problem.

Page 52

Answer Key

Page 53

Fact Search

Fly through the heavens and circle the hidden multiplication sentences. Add an **x** sign and an **=** sign.

A. 1 (0 × 2 = 0) 1
B. (3 × 1 = 3) 2 5
C. 2 (2 × 7 = 14) 2
D. 1 4 (8 × 2 = 16)
E. (0 × 5 = 0) 3 3
F. 12 (6 × 2 = 12) 6
G. 1 0 (1 × 1 = 1)
H. 10 (5 × 2 = 10) 12
I. 1 9 (0 × 9 = 0)
J. (9 × 2 = 18) 6 2

K. 14 7 (7 × 1 = 7)
L. 2 5 (0 × 10 = 0)
M. (2 × 4 = 8) 4 12
N. 4 (2 × 2 = 4) 6
O. 0 1 (5 × 1 = 5)
P. (4 × 0 = 0) 2 4
Q. 2 11 (2 × 11 = 22)
R. 8 (1 × 9 = 9) 18
S. (6 × 1 = 6) 2 8
T. 7 (7 × 0 = 0) 7
U. (3 × 2 = 6) 3 3
V. 7 1 (8 × 1 = 8)
W. (12 × 2 = 24) 2 6
X. (8 × 0 = 0) 4 2
Y. 6 (1 × 2 = 2) 12
Z. (10 × 2 = 20) 10 1

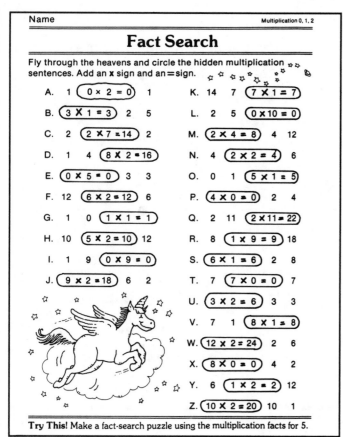

Try This! Make a fact-search puzzle using the multiplication facts for 5.

Page 53

Page 54

Multiplication Puzzle

Fix this mixed-up puzzle. First cut out the puzzle pieces. Then put the puzzle together by matching each multiplication problem with its correct answer. Glue the finished puzzle on another sheet of paper.

Example: 3 × 5 = | 15

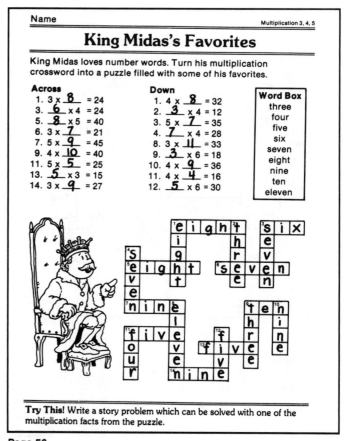

5 x 4 = 20	8 x 4 = 32	
6 x 3 =	9 x 4 =	2 x 4 =
18	36	8
7 x 3 = 21	8 x 5 = 40	
7 x 4 =	3 x 5 =	7 x 2 =
28	15	14
3 x 2 = 6	9 x 3 = 27	

Page 54

Page 55

Munch a Bunch

Munch through these super subs. Fill in each ◯ with the number that makes the number sentence true.

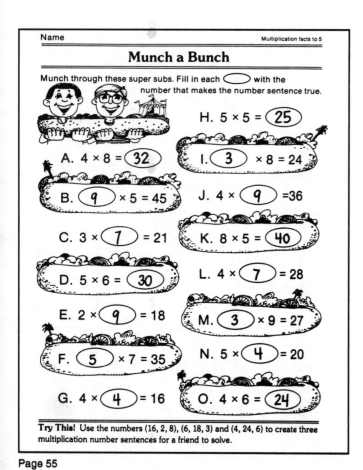

A. 4 × 8 = (32)
B. (9) × 5 = 45
C. 3 × (7) = 21
D. 5 × 6 = (30)
E. 2 × (9) = 18
F. (5) × 7 = 35
G. 4 × (4) = 16

H. 5 × 5 = (25)
I. (3) × 8 = 24
J. 4 × (9) = 36
K. 8 × 5 = (40)
L. 4 × (7) = 28
M. (3) × 9 = 27
N. 5 × (4) = 20
O. 4 × 6 = (24)

Try This! Use the numbers (16, 2, 8), (6, 18, 3) and (4, 24, 6) to create three multiplication number sentences for a friend to solve.

Page 55

Page 56

King Midas's Favorites

King Midas loves number words. Turn his multiplication crossword into a puzzle filled with some of his favorites.

Across
1. 3 x **8** = 24
3. **6** x 4 = 24
5. **8** x 5 = 40
6. 3 x **7** = 21
7. 5 x **9** = 45
9. 4 x **10** = 40
11. 5 x **5** = 25
13. **5** x 3 = 15
14. 3 x **9** = 27

Down
1. 4 x **8** = 32
2. **3** x 4 = 12
3. 5 x **7** = 35
4. **7** x 4 = 28
8. 3 x **11** = 33
9. **3** x 6 = 18
10. 4 x **9** = 36
11. 4 x **4** = 16
12. **5** x 6 = 30

Word Box
three
four
five
six
seven
eight
nine
ten
eleven

Try This! Write a story problem which can be solved with one of the multiplication facts from the puzzle.

Page 56

Answer Key

Name_____   Skill: Multiplication facts

Multiplication Secret Code

Fill in each box with the
number that solves the
multiplication math sentence.

$2 \times 5 = \boxed{10}$ $9 \times 2 = \boxed{18}$ $9 \times \boxed{^R 9} = 81$

$4 \times \boxed{^B 4} = 16$ $\boxed{^L 3} \times 4 = 12$ $\boxed{^S 5} \times 7 = 35$

$3 \times 9 = \boxed{27}$ $5 \times \boxed{^M 7} = 35$ $5 \times 5 = \boxed{25}$

$\boxed{^E 6} \times 5 = 30$ $8 \times 3 = \boxed{24}$ $8 \times \boxed{^U 1} = 8$

$7 \times 4 = \boxed{28}$ $7 \times \boxed{^O 8} = 56$ $\boxed{^W 2} \times 6 = 12$

$3 \times \boxed{^H 0} = 0$ $4 \times 5 = \boxed{20}$ $6 \times 6 = \boxed{36}$

Use the code to solve these riddles. Write the letter from the box that
matches the numbers.

1. What has a tongue but cannot talk?

   <u>a</u> <u>s</u> <u>h</u> <u>o</u> <u>e</u>
   10 5 0 8 6

2. What has feathers but does not squawk?

   <u>a</u> <u>p</u> <u>i</u> <u>l</u> <u>l</u> <u>o</u> <u>w</u>
   10 20 18 3 3 8 2

3. What has legs but cannot walk?

   <u>a</u> <u>t</u> <u>a</u> <u>b</u> <u>l</u> <u>e</u> <u>o</u> <u>r</u> <u>c</u> <u>h</u> <u>a</u> <u>i</u> <u>r</u>
   10 25 10 4 3 6 8 9 27 0 10 18 9

Brainwork! Write three multiplication problems whose answer is 12.

Page 57

Name_____   Skill: Addition, Subtraction, Multiplication

A Day at the Park

Use this picture to work each problem below. Write numbers on the lines.
Write the addition, subtraction, or multiplication signs in the circles. Then
mark the final answer in the box.

1. Begin with the total number of
children. Multiply by the number of
boys. Subtract the number of girls.

   $4 \,\textcircled{\times}\, 2 = \underline{8}$
   $8 \,\textcircled{-}\, 2 = \boxed{6}$

2. Begin with the number of flowers.
Subtract the number of children.
Multiply by the number of trees.

   $8 \,\textcircled{-}\, 4 = \underline{4}$
   $4 \,\textcircled{\times}\, 6 = \boxed{24}$

3. Begin with the number of bicycles.
Add the number of park benches.
Multiply by the number of swings.

   $2 \,\textcircled{+}\, 1 = \underline{3}$
   $3 \,\textcircled{\times}\, 3 = \boxed{9}$

4. Begin with the number of dogs.
Add the number of birds. Multiply
by the number of cats.

   $2 \,\textcircled{+}\, 3 = \underline{5}$
   $5 \,\textcircled{\times}\, 1 = \boxed{5}$

Brainwork! Write your own math problem using objects from the picture.

Page 58

Name_____   Multiplication, division 2s, 3s

Mr. Magician's Hat Tricks

This array of X's shows these facts.

X X X	$4 \times 3 = 12$
X X X	$3 \times 4 = 12$
X X X	$12 \div 4 = 3$
X X X	$12 \div 3 = 4$

Write **two multiplication facts** and **two
division facts** shown by the things Mr.
Magician has pulled out of his hat.

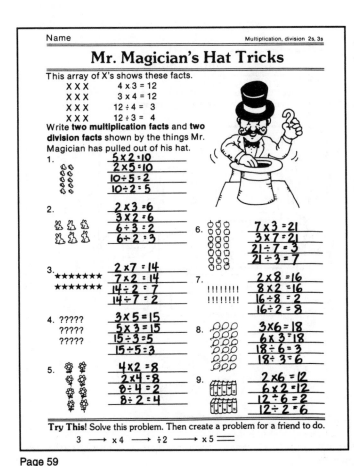

1.
   $5 \times 2 = 10$
   $2 \times 5 = 10$
   $10 \div 5 = 2$
   $10 \div 2 = 5$

2.
   $2 \times 3 = 6$
   $3 \times 2 = 6$
   $6 \div 3 = 2$
   $6 \div 2 = 3$

3.
   $2 \times 7 = 14$
   $7 \times 2 = 14$
   $14 \div 2 = 7$
   $14 \div 7 = 2$

4.
   $3 \times 5 = 15$
   $5 \times 3 = 15$
   $15 \div 3 = 5$
   $15 \div 5 = 3$

5.
   $4 \times 2 = 8$
   $2 \times 4 = 8$
   $8 \div 4 = 2$
   $8 \div 2 = 4$

6.
   $7 \times 3 = 21$
   $3 \times 7 = 21$
   $21 \div 7 = 3$
   $21 \div 3 = 7$

7.
   $2 \times 8 = 16$
   $8 \times 2 = 16$
   $16 \div 8 = 2$
   $16 \div 2 = 8$

8.
   $3 \times 6 = 18$
   $6 \times 3 = 18$
   $18 \div 6 = 3$
   $18 \div 3 = 6$

9.
   $2 \times 6 = 12$
   $6 \times 2 = 12$
   $12 \div 6 = 2$
   $12 \div 2 = 6$

Try This! Solve this problem. Then create a problem for a friend to do.

$3 \longrightarrow \times 4 \longrightarrow \div 2 \longrightarrow \times 5 \underline{\quad\quad}$

Page 59

Name_____   <u>Picture should be colored.</u>   Drawing segments

Circus Segments

A straight line drawn between two points is called a **segment**.
Use a ruler to draw each segment. Then color the picture.

1. segment AB ($\overline{AB}$)
2. segment BC ($\overline{BC}$)
3. segment CD ($\overline{CD}$)
4. segment DE ($\overline{DE}$)
5. segment FJ ($\overline{FJ}$)
6. segment GK ($\overline{GK}$)
7. segment HL ($\overline{HL}$)
8. segment IM ($\overline{IM}$)
9. segment NR ($\overline{NR}$)
10. segment OS ($\overline{OS}$)
11. segment PT ($\overline{PT}$)
12. segment QU ($\overline{QU}$)
13. segment VW ($\overline{VW}$)
14. segment XY ($\overline{XY}$)
15. segment VY ($\overline{VY}$)
16. segment XW ($\overline{XW}$)

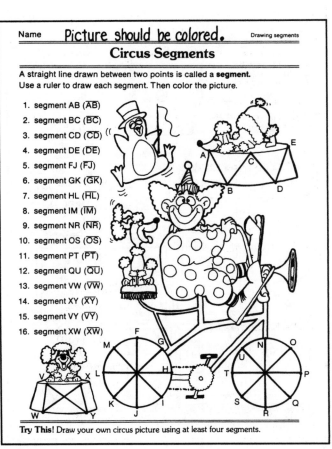

Try This! Draw your own circus picture using at least four segments.

Page 60

Answer Key

Corners and Sides

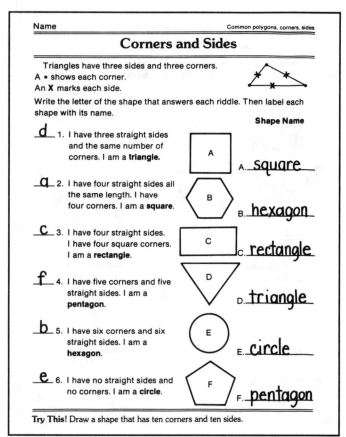

Triangles have three sides and three corners.
A • shows each corner.
An **X** marks each side.

Write the letter of the shape that answers each riddle. Then label each shape with its name.

Shape Name

__d__ 1. I have three straight sides and the same number of corners. I am a **triangle**.

A. square

__a__ 2. I have four straight sides all the same length. I have four corners. I am a **square**.

B. hexagon

__c__ 3. I have four straight sides. I have four square corners. I am a **rectangle**.

C. rectangle

__f__ 4. I have five corners and five straight sides. I am a **pentagon**.

D. triangle

__b__ 5. I have six corners and six straight sides. I am a **hexagon**.

E. circle

__e__ 6. I have no straight sides and no corners. I am a **circle**.

F. pentagon

Try This! Draw a shape that has ten corners and ten sides.

Page 61

Geometric Dinosaurs

Brighten up these dinosaurs!
Color all triangles (△) green.
Color all rectangles (▭) purple.
Color all circles (○) blue.
Color the remaining parts brown.

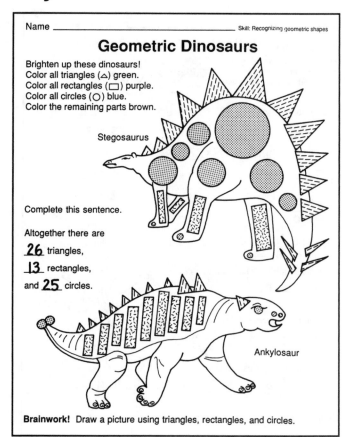

Stegosaurus

Complete this sentence.

Altogether there are

26 triangles,

13 rectangles,

and **25** circles.

Ankylosaur

Brainwork! Draw a picture using triangles, rectangles, and circles.

Page 62

Sorting Shapes

Look at these shapes.

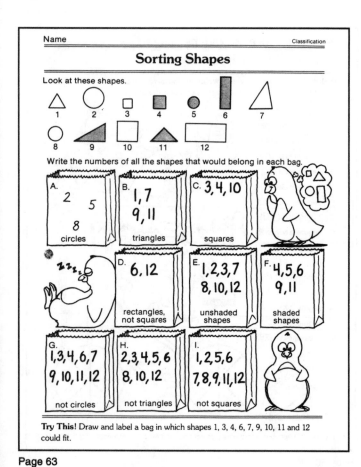

1 2 3 4 5 6 7

8 9 10 11 12

Write the numbers of all the shapes that would belong in each bag.

A. 2 5 8
circles

B. 1, 7 9, 11
triangles

C. 3, 4, 10
squares

D. 6, 12
rectangles, not squares

E. 1, 2, 3, 7 8, 10, 12
unshaded shapes

F. 4, 5, 6 9, 11
shaded shapes

G. 1, 3, 4, 6, 7 9, 10, 11, 12
not circles

H. 2, 3, 4, 5, 6 8, 10, 12
not triangles

I. 1, 2, 5, 6 7, 8, 9, 11, 12
not squares

Try This! Draw and label a bag in which shapes 1, 3, 4, 6, 7, 9, 10, 11 and 12 could fit.

Page 63

Same Shapes

Cut out and arrange the pieces on the grid so:
• each piece shares a side with another piece that has the same shape
• each column (down) has more than two different shapes.
Glue the pieces in place.

Layouts will vary.

Page 64

Answer Key

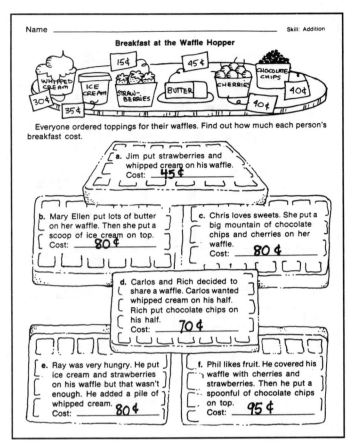

Page 65

Skill: Addition

Breakfast at the Waffle Hopper

Everyone ordered toppings for their waffles. Find out how much each person's breakfast cost.

a. Jim put strawberries and whipped cream on his waffle. Cost: **45¢**

b. Mary Ellen put lots of butter on her waffle. Then she put a scoop of ice cream on top. Cost: **80¢**

c. Chris loves sweets. She put a big mountain of chocolate chips and cherries on her waffle. Cost: **80¢**

d. Carlos and Rich decided to share a waffle. Carlos wanted whipped cream on his half. Rich put chocolate chips on his half. Cost: **70¢**

e. Ray was very hungry. He put ice cream and strawberries on his waffle but that wasn't enough. He added a pile of whipped cream. Cost: **80¢**

f. Phil likes fruit. He covered his waffle with cherries and strawberries. Then he put a spoonful of chocolate chips on top. Cost: **95¢**

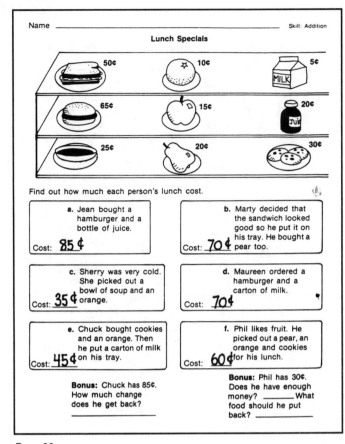

Page 66

Skill: Addition

Lunch Specials

Find out how much each person's lunch cost.

a. Jean bought a hamburger and a bottle of juice. Cost: **85¢**

b. Marty decided that the sandwich looked good so he put it on his tray. He bought a pear too. Cost: **70¢**

c. Sherry was very cold. She picked out a bowl of soup and an orange. Cost: **35¢**

d. Maureen ordered a hamburger and a carton of milk. Cost: **70¢**

e. Chuck bought cookies and an orange. Then he put a carton of milk on his tray. Cost: **45¢**

f. Phil likes fruit. He picked out a pear, an orange and cookies for his lunch. Cost: **60¢**

Bonus: Chuck has 85¢. How much change does he get back? _____

Bonus: Phil has 30¢. Does he have enough money? _____ What food should he put back? _____

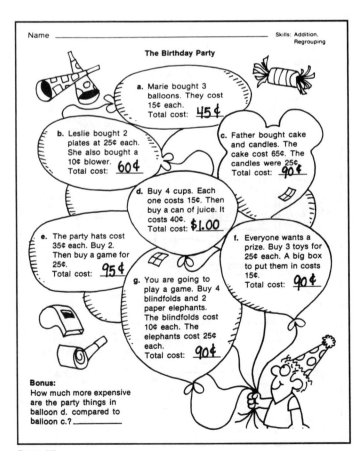

Page 67

Skills: Addition, Regrouping

The Birthday Party

a. Marie bought 3 balloons. They cost 15¢ each. Total cost: **45¢**

b. Leslie bought 2 plates at 25¢ each. She also bought a 10¢ blower. Total cost: **60¢**

c. Father bought cake and candles. The cake cost 65¢. The candles were 25¢. Total cost: **90¢**

d. Buy 4 cups. Each one costs 15¢. Then buy a can of juice. It costs 40¢. Total cost: **$1.00**

e. The party hats cost 35¢ each. Buy 2. Then buy a game for 25¢. Total cost: **95¢**

f. Everyone wants a prize. Buy 3 toys for 25¢ each. A big box to put them in costs 15¢. Total cost: **90¢**

g. You are going to play a game. Buy 4 blindfolds and 2 paper elephants. The blindfolds cost 10¢ each. The elephants cost 25¢ each. Total cost: **90¢**

Bonus: How much more expensive are the party things in balloon d. compared to balloon c.? _____

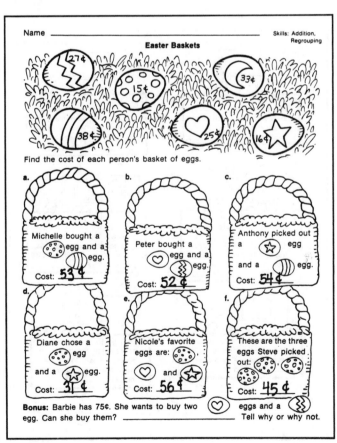

Page 68

Skills: Addition, Regrouping

Easter Baskets

Find the cost of each person's basket of eggs.

a. Michelle bought a egg and a egg. Cost: **53¢**

b. Peter bought a egg and a egg. Cost: **52¢**

c. Anthony picked out a egg and a egg. Cost: **54¢**

d. Diane chose a egg and a egg. Cost: **31¢**

e. Nicole's favorite eggs are: and Cost: **56¢**

f. These are the three eggs Steve picked out: Cost: **45¢**

Bonus: Barbie has 75¢. She wants to buy two egg. Can she buy them? _____ Tell why or why not.

© Frank Schaffer Publications, Inc.

121

FS-32021 Math Activities

Answer Key

Page 69

Page 70

Page 71

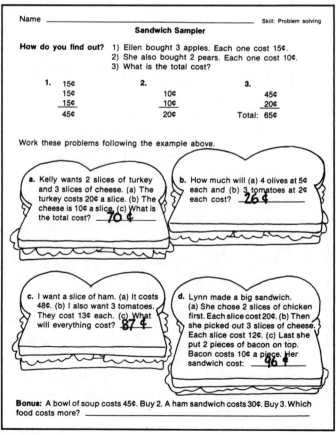

Page 72

122

FS-32021 Math Activities

Answer Key

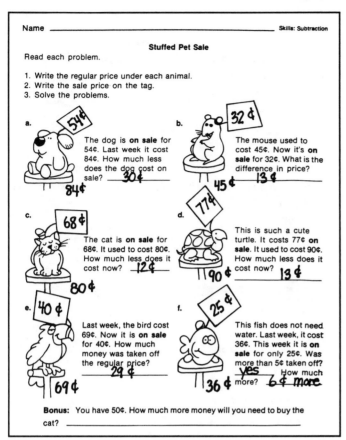

Page 73

Page 74

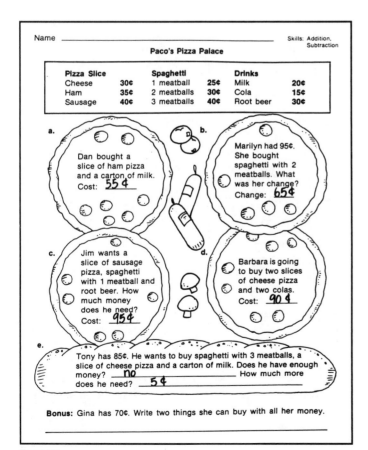

Page 75

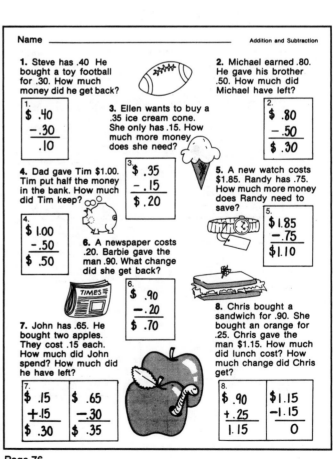

Page 76

FS-32021 Math Activities

Answer Key

Page 77

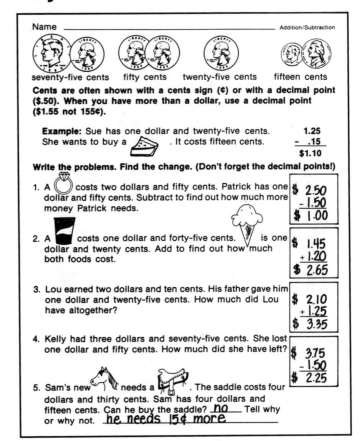

Page 78

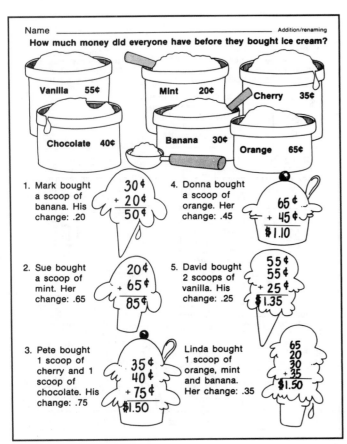

Page 79

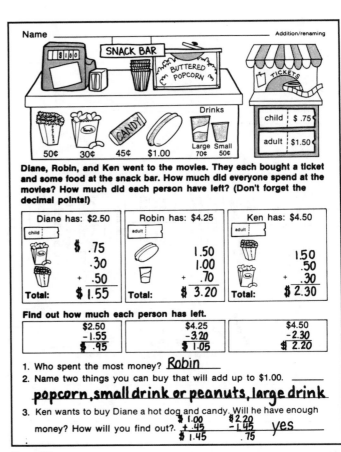

Page 80

124

FS-32021 Math Activities

Answer Key

Write the number sentence and label your answer.

1. Mike had $6.91. He bought a shirt. How much did he have left?

$6.91 - 5.87 = 1.04$

Mike had $1.04 left.

2. Linda bought the skirt. If she gave the sales person $9.70, how much change did she get?

$9.70 - 7.42 = 2.28$

Linda got $2.28 change.

3. Jim's dad gave him $9.25. If Jim bought the pants, how much money will his dad get back?

$9.25 - 6.73 = 2.52$

He will get back $2.52.

4. Mark bought the boy's hat. If he started with $4.50, how much does he have left?

$4.50 - 3.69 = .81$

Mark had $.81 left.

5. Ann's mother had $9.79. If Ann buys the blouse, how much change will her mother get?

$9.79 - 8.69 = 1.10$

She will get $1.10 change.

6. If Nancy buys the girl's hat, how much change will she get from a $5.00 bill?

$5.00 - 2.88 = 2.12$

Nancy will get $2.12 change.

Page 83

Morry's Shoe Sale

a. I am going to the beach this summer. Three pairs of flip-flops would be great! How much will they cost? $10.50

b. Tom wants to buy a pair of Martian shoes. His mother will give him $8.50. How much money will Tom have to add? $1.50

c. Kerri will buy 2 pairs of boots. How much money will she save when she buys them on sale? $4.90

d. Find out which pair of shoes was reduced more in price—the saddle shoes or the boots. saddle shoes

Bonus: Scott bought a pair of boots at another store for $12.95. How much would he have saved if he had bought them at Morry's?

e. Mom bought 2 pairs of Martian shoes. How much did she save when she bought them on sale? $5.00

Page 86

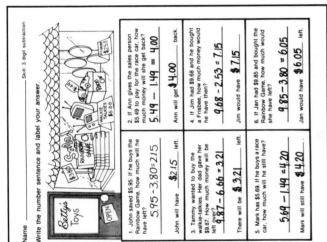

Write the number sentence and label your answer.

Betty's Toys

1. John saved $5.95. If he buys the Rainbow Game, how much will he have left?

$5.95 - 3.80 = 2.15$

John will have $2.15 left.

2. If Ann gives the sales person $5.49 to pay for the race car, how much money will she get back?

$5.49 - 1.49 = 4.00$

Ann will get $4.00 back.

3. Tammy wanted to buy the walkie-talkies. Her dad gave her $9.87. How much money will be left over?

$9.87 - 6.66 = 3.21$

There will be $3.21 left.

4. If Jim had $9.68 and he bought a Frisbee, how much money would he have then?

$9.68 - 2.53 = 7.15$

Jim would have $7.15.

5. Mark has $5.69. If he buys a race car, how much will he still have?

$5.69 - 1.49 = 4.20$

Mark will still have $4.20.

6. If Jan had $9.85 and bought the Rainbow Game, how much would she have left?

$9.85 - 3.80 = 6.05$

Jan would have $6.05 left.

Page 82

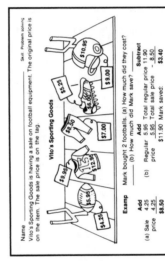

Vito's Sporting Goods is having a sale on football equipment. The original price is on the item. The sale price is on the tag.

Vito's Sporting Goods

Example

Mark bought 2 footballs. (a) How much did they cost? (b) How much did Mark save?

	Add		Subtract
(a) Sale	5.95	(b) Total regular price	11.90
price	5.95	Total sale price	−8.50
	$11.90	Mark saved:	$3.40

a. Coach Benson bought 3 pairs of shoes. How much did they cost? $15.75 How much money did he save? $2.25

$$\begin{array}{r} Add \\ 4.25 \\ 4.25 \\ \hline \$8.50 \end{array}$$

b. Pam and Patty are twins. Pam bought 2 shirts. Patty bought 2 helmets. How much did Pam spend? $19.90 How much did Patty spend? $18.00 How much did Pam save? $6.00 How much did Patty save? $3.90

c. Our team wants to buy 3 helmets. How much will they cost? $27.00 How much will the team save? $5.85

d. Dad bought me 3 footballs. How much did they cost? $12.75 How much did he save? $5.10

Bonus: The team has $40.00. After buying the helmets, how much change did they have? $13.00 Name two other items the team can buy with their change.

Page 85

How much did each girl spend on food? How much change was left?

Kate bought peanuts and popcorn.

$$\begin{array}{r} Add \\ \$.85 \\ +\ .75 \\ \hline \$1.60 \end{array} \qquad \begin{array}{r} Subtract \\ \$2.85 \\ -1.60 \\ \hline \$1.25 \end{array}$$

Tina bought a soda, cookies and went to the magic show.

$$\begin{array}{r} Add \\ \$.50 \\ .50 \\ +1.50 \\ \hline \$2.50 \end{array} \qquad \begin{array}{r} Subtract \\ \$3.90 \\ -2.50 \\ \hline \$1.40 \end{array}$$

Sharon took a pony ride and ate some cookies.

$$\begin{array}{r} Add \\ \$1.00 \\ +\ .50 \\ \hline \$1.50 \end{array} \qquad \begin{array}{r} Subtract \\ \$3.00 \\ -2.00 \\ \hline \$1.00 \end{array}$$

Peggy went to the magic show! Later, she got a soda.

$$\begin{array}{r} Add \\ \$1.50 \\ +\ .50 \\ \hline \$2.00 \end{array} \qquad \begin{array}{r} Subtract \\ \$3.75 \\ -1.50 \\ \hline \$2.25 \end{array}$$

1. Who has the most money left over? **Sharon**

2. Name two things Peggy could buy with her change. **soda, cookies**

3. Can Kate go to the magic show? Tell why or why not. **no She needs 25¢ more**

Page 81

Write the number sentence and label your answer.

1. Andy made $2.75 on Saturday and $3.25 on Sunday. How much did he make altogether?

$2.75 + 3.25 = 6.00$

Andy made $6.00.

2. Mike saved $7.82. He spent $4.95 on a gift for his brother. How much did he have left?

$7.82 - 4.95 = 2.87$

Mike had $2.87 left.

3. Susan spent $6.84 on a gift for her mother and $1.77 to get it wrapped. How much did they spend in all?

$6.84 + 1.77 = 8.61$

Susan spent $8.61 in all.

4. Bob bought 3 toys. One was $1.49, another was $2.37, and the third was $.38. What was the total?

$1.49 + 2.37 + .38 = 4.24$

Total cost was $4.24.

5. Mary had $9.00. She paid $2.64 for her sister's birthday gift. How much did she have then?

$9.00 - 2.64 = 6.36$

Mary had $6.36 then.

6. Jack had $3.49. On the way to the store, he lost $.27. How much can he spend now?

$3.49 - .27 = 3.22$

Jack can spend $3.22 now.

7. If Linda started with $8.70 and spent $1.57 on her baby sister, how much money does she have left?

$8.70 - 1.57 = 7.13$

Linda has $7.13 left.

Page 84

Answer Key

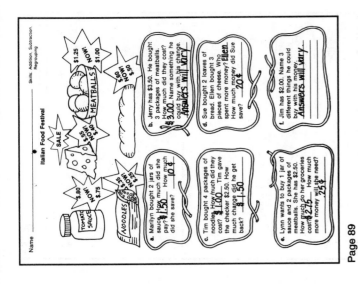

Page 87

Name _____

Trick or Treat

Skill: 3-digit addition, Subtraction, Regrouping

It's Halloween! Six children went to the party store to pick out their costumes. Find out how much each child spent. Find out how much change each person got back.

a. Sam... bought a mask and a cape. He had $7.00.
Spent: $3.10 Change: $3.90

b. Susan... bought wings and a crown. She had $4.25.
Spent: $2.45 Change: $1.80

c. Robin... bought rabbit ears and teeth. She had $5.50.
Spent: $4.75 Change: $.75

d. Matt... bought a mask, a halo and shoes. He had $5.75.
Spent: $4.10 Change: $1.65

Bonus: Who has enough change to buy a mask and a halo?

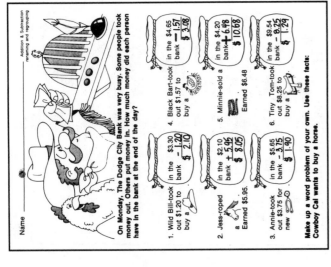

Page 88

Name _____

Addition & Subtraction renaming and regrouping

On Monday, The Dodge City Bank was very busy. Some people took money out. Others put money in. How much money did each person have in the bank at the end of the day?

1. Wild Bill—took out $1.20 to buy a ____
   in the $3.30 bank −1.20 $2.10

2. Jess—roped a ____
   Earned $5.95.
   in the $2.10 bank +5.95 $8.05

3. Annie—took out $3.75 for new ____
   in the $5.65 bank −3.75 $1.90

4. Black Bart—took out $1.57 to buy a ____
   in the $4.65 bank −1.57 $3.08

5. Minnie—sold a ____
   Earned $6.48
   in the $4.20 bank +6.48 $10.68

6. Tiny Tom—took out $8.25 to buy a ____
   in the $9.54 bank −8.25 $1.29

Make up a word problem of your own. Use these facts: Cowboy Cal wants to buy a horse.

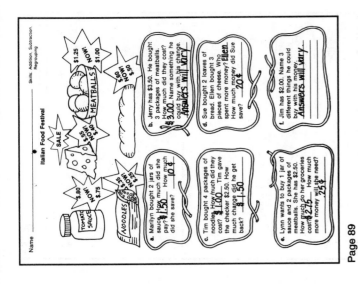

Page 89

Name _____

Italian Food Festival

Skills: Addition, Subtraction, Regrouping

a. Marilyn bought 2 jars of sauce. How much did she pay? $1.50 How much did she save? 10¢

b. Jerry has $3.50. He bought 3 packages of meatballs. How much did they cost? $3.00 Name something he could buy with his change. Answers will vary.

c. Tim bought 4 packages of noodles. How much did it cost? $1.00 Tim gave the checker $2.50. How much change did he get back? $1.50

d. Sue bought 2 loaves of bread. Ellen bought 3 pieces of cheese. Who spent more money? Ellen How much money did Sue save? 20¢

e. Lynn wants to buy 1 jar of sauce and 2 packages of meatballs. She has $2.50. How much do her groceries cost? $2.75 How much more money will she need? 25¢

f. Jim has $2.00. Name 3 different things he could buy with his money. Answers will vary.

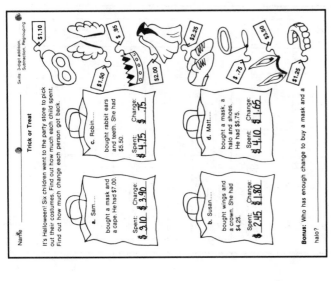

Page 90

Name _____

Maude's Giant Cookies

Skills: Addition and subtraction Subtraction, Regrouping

EXAMPLE
Larry wants to buy 2 trees and a heart. He has $2.40. Can he buy the cookies?
What will be his change?
Larry's money $2.40
Cost of cookies −1.80
Change $.60

$.65
.65
1.30
+.50
$1.80

a. Terry has $2.50. He wants to buy 2 gingerbread men and a star. Can he buy them? no Tell why or why not. They only cost $2.40 and Terry only had $2.50

b. Mary gave 3 trees to Sharon. She gave 2 stars to Sue. Which cookies cost more? 3 trees How much more? $.35

c. Jeff has $4.35. Phil has $3.45. Which boy can buy exactly 3 trees and 3 hearts with his money? Phil

d. At the end of the day, Maude gives away leftover cookies. Joe paid Maude $1.60. He had 4 stars. How many did he get free? 2

e. Maude put these cookies in packages: 3 stars in one package, 3 trees in another package, and 4 hearts in the last package. How much did each package cost? $1.80 What was the total cost of all the cookies? $5.55

f. The gingerbread men are going to be on sale for $.90 each. Jan has $2.75. Can she buy 3 gingerbread men? no Can she buy a star too? yes

g. Cory bought 6 hearts. They were all broken so he only paid half price. How much did the cookies cost? $1.50

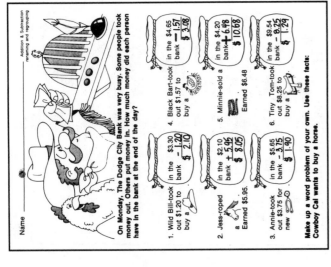

Page 91

Name _____

Ice Cream Match-Up

Skill: Multiplication

Example: Tim bought 4 cones. The total cost was 20¢. How much did each cone cost? This is how you find out. 4 × ___ = 20¢ Do you know your multiplication tables? If so, the answer will be easy for you to figure out.

Find each child's matching cone. Write his or her name on the line under the correct cone.

a. Cathy b. Helen c. Donna d. Marie e. Sara f. Dick g. Dave

Dave bought 3 cones. The total cost was 21¢.

Marie bought 6 cones. The total cost was 24¢.

Sara bought 2 cones. The total cost was 18¢.

Donna bought 5 cones. The total cost was 10¢.

Dick bought 5 cones. The total cost was 25¢.

Helen bought 3 cones. The total cost was 9¢.

Cathy bought 5 cones. The total cost was 40¢.

Bonus: Don has 27¢. He wants to buy 3 ice cream cones. How much will each one cost?

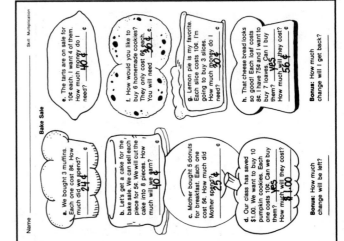

Page 92

Name _____

Bake Sale

Skill: Multiplication

a. We bought 3 muffins. Each one cost 8¢. How much did we spend? 24¢

b. Let's get a cake for the bake sale. We can sell each piece for 5¢. We will cut the cake into 8 pieces. How much will we earn? 40¢

c. Mother bought 5 donuts for breakfast. Each one cost 5¢. How much did Mother spend? 25¢

d. Our class has saved $1.00. We want to buy 10 pumpkin cookies. Each one costs 10¢. Can we buy them? yes How much will they cost? $1.00

e. The tarts are on sale for 10¢ each. I want 4 of them. How much money do I need? 40¢

f. How would you like to buy 6 homemade cookies? They only cost 5¢ each. 30¢

g. Lemon pie is my favorite. Each slice costs 10¢. How much money do I need? 20¢

h. That cheese bread looks so good! Each loaf costs 8¢. I have 75¢ and I want to buy 7 loaves. Can I buy them? yes How much will they cost? 56¢

Bonus: How much change will I get back?

FS-32021 Math Activities

Answer Key

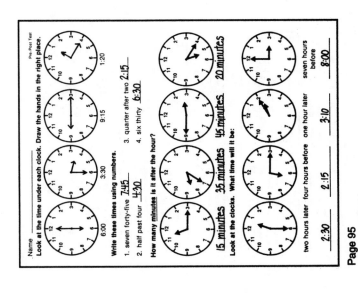

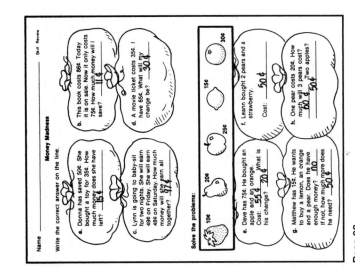

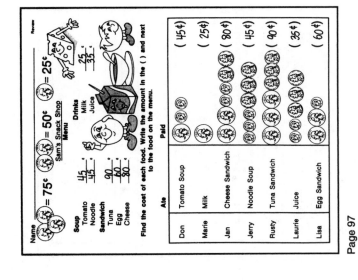

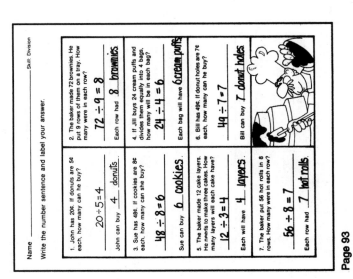

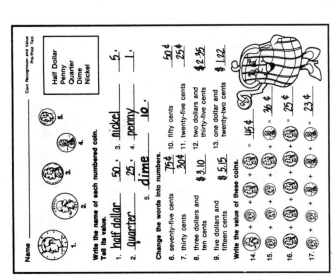

Answer Key

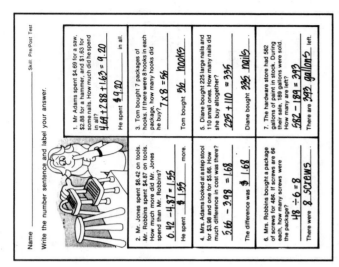

Name _____
Write the number sentence and label your answer.

1. Mr. Adams spent $4.69 for a saw, $2.88 for a hammer, and $1.63 for some nails. How much did he spend in all?
4.69 + 2.88 + 1.63 = 9.20
He spent $9.20 in all.

2. Mr. Jones spent $6.42 on tools. Mr. Robbins spent $4.87 on tools. How much more did Mr. Jones spend than Mr. Robbins?
6.42 - 4.87 = 1.55
He spent $1.55 more.

3. Tom bought 7 packages of hooks. If there were 8 hooks in each package, how many hooks did he buy?
7 x 8 = 56
Tom bought 56 hooks.

4. Mrs. Adams looked at a step stool for $3.98 and one for $5.66. How much difference in cost was there?
5.66 - 3.98 = 1.68
The difference was $1.68.

5. Diane bought 225 large nails and 110 small ones. How many nails did she buy altogether?
225 + 110 = 335
Diane bought 335 nails.

6. Mrs. Robbins bought a package of screws for 48¢. If screws are 6¢ each, how many screws were in the package?
48 ÷ 6 = 8
There were 8 screws.

7. The hardware store had 582 gallons of paint in stock. During their sale, 189 gallons were sold. How many are left?
582 - 189 = 393
There are 393 gallons left.

Page 101

The Math Box Game

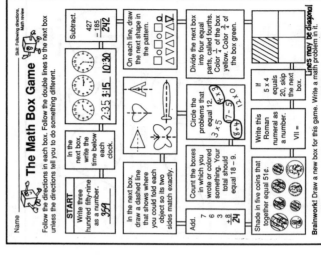

Name _____

Follow the directions in each box. Follow the double lines to the next box unless the directions tell you to do something different.

START — Write three hundred fifty-nine as a number. 359

In the next box, write the time below each clock. 2:35 3:15 10:30

Subtract. 427 − 185 = 242

On each line, draw the next equal shape in the pattern.

In the next box, draw a dashed line that shows where you could fold each object so its two sides match exactly.

Circle the problems that equal 12.
3 x 5   (4 x 3)
(7 − 5)   (6 + 6)

Divide the next box into four equal parts, called fourths. Color 1/4 of the box yellow. Color 1/2 of the box green.

Add. 7, 6, 3, +8 = 24

Count the boxes in which you wrote or colored something. Your total should equal 18 − 9.

Write this Roman numeral as a number. VII =

Shade in five coins that together equal 51¢.

If 5 x 4 equals 20, skip the next box.

Brainwork! Draw a new box for this game. Write a math problem in it.
Lines may be diagonal

Page 104

Jim's Restaurant

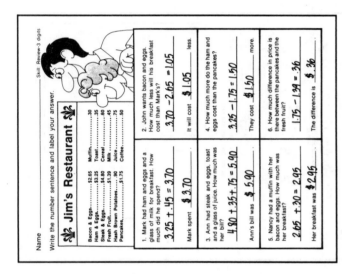

Name _____
Write the number sentence and label your answer.

Menu	
Bacon & Eggs.........$2.65	Muffin.........30
Ham & Eggs..........$3.25	Toast..........35
Steak & Eggs.........$4.80	Cereal.........60
Fresh Fruit..........$1.39	Milk...........45
Hash Brown Potatoes....90	Juice..........75
Pancakes............$1.75	Coffee.........50

1. Mark had ham and eggs and a glass of milk for breakfast. How much did he spend?
3.25 + .45 = 3.70
Mark spent $3.70.

2. John wants bacon and eggs. How much less will his breakfast cost than Mark's?
3.70 − 2.65 = 1.05
It will cost $1.05 less.

3. Ann had steak and eggs, toast and a glass of juice. How much was her bill?
4.80 + .35 + .75 = 5.90
Ann's bill was $5.90.

4. How much more do the ham and eggs cost than the pancakes?
3.25 − 1.75 = 1.50
They cost $1.50 more.

5. Nancy had a muffin with her bacon and eggs. How much was her breakfast?
2.65 + .30 = 2.95
Her breakfast was $2.95.

6. How much difference in price is there between the pancakes and the fresh fruit?
1.75 − 1.39 = .36
The difference is $.36.

Page 100

Math Path

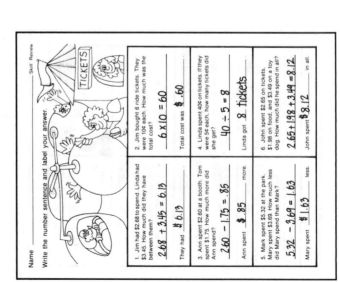

Name _____

Follow the directions in each box. Follow the arrow to the next box unless the directions tell you to do something different.

START — Add. 27 +36 = 63

Fill in the missing numbers.
5, 10, 15, 20, 25, 30, 35, 40, 45, 50, 55, 60, 65

Color 1/2 of the next box blue. Color 1/2 of the box red.

Circle all the odd numbers in this box.
3 4 (13) 12 (7)
(27) (9) 8 (25) 20

Write the number in the box that makes the math sentence correct. 12 − 8 = 4

What is the largest number you can write using the digits 7, 2, and 9 once? 972

Write ninety-five as a number. 95

How many quarters equal one dollar?

Subtract. .57 − .40 = .17

Count the boxes in which you wrote or colored something. Your total should equal 6 + 3.

In the next box, color the squares green. Color the triangles orange. Color the rectangles purple.

If 82 is larger than 79, skip the next box.

Brainwork! Draw a new box to add to the path. Write a math problem in it.

Page 103

Name _____
Write the number sentence and label your answer.

May I take your order, please?

Menu	
16 oz Steak	$4.58
Italian Spaghetti	$2.24
Salad	$1.43
Hamburger	$1.32
Milk	.31
Coffee	.40

1. Dad had steak and a cup of coffee for dinner. How much did she spend?
4.58 + .40 = 4.98
Dad's bill was $4.98.

2. Mom had the spaghetti and a salad. How much did she spend?
2.24 + 1.43 = 3.67
Mom spent $3.67.

3. John had $3.68. If he bought a hamburger, how much did he have left?
3.68 − 1.32 = 2.36
John had $2.36 left.

4. Sue had a salad and a glass of milk. If she left a 25¢ tip, how much did she spend?
1.43 + .31 + .25 = 1.99
Sue spent $1.99.

5. How much more did Dad's dinner cost than Mom's?
4.98 − 3.67 = 1.31
It cost $1.31 more.

6. How much difference in price is there between the steak dinner and the spaghetti dinner?
4.58 − 2.24 = 2.34
A difference of $2.34.

Page 99

Name _____
Write the number sentence and label your answer.

TICKETS

1. Jim had $2.68 to spend. Linda had $3.45. How much did they have between them?
2.68 + 3.45 = 6.13
They had $6.13.

2. Jim bought 6 ride tickets. They were 10¢ each. How much was the total cost?
6 x 10 = 60
Total cost was $.60.

3. Ann spent $2.60 at a booth. Tom spent $1.75. How much more did Ann spend?
2.60 − 1.75 = .85
Ann spent $.85 more.

4. Linda spent 40¢ on tickets. If they were 5¢ each, how many tickets did she get?
40 ÷ 5 = 8
Linda got 8 tickets.

5. Mary spent $5.32 at the park. Mark spent $3.69. How much less did Mary spend than Mark?
5.32 − 3.69 = 1.63
Mary spent $1.63 less.

6. John spent $2.65 on tickets, $1.98 on food, and $3.49 on a toy dog. How much did he spend in all?
2.65 + 1.98 + 3.49 = 8.12
John spent $8.12 in all.

Page 102